IMAGES
of America

TULSA
THE WAR YEARS

IMAGES
of America

TULSA
THE WAR YEARS

Mike Buckendorf

ARCADIA
PUBLISHING

Copyright © 2011 by Mike Buckendorf
ISBN 978-0-7385-9052-3

Published by Arcadia Publishing
Charleston, South Carolina

Printed in the United States of America

Library of Congress Control Number: 2011940519

For all general information, please contact Arcadia Publishing:
Telephone 843-853-2070
Fax 843-853-0044
E-mail sales@arcadiapublishing.com
For customer service and orders:
Toll-Free 1-888-313-2665

Visit us on the Internet at www.arcadiapublishing.com

*Dedicated to the millions who served and those
who now live on only in our memories*

CONTENTS

ACKNOWLEDGMENTS

There are several people I would like to thank for aiding me in producing this work. First and foremost, I'd like to thank my parents, Mike Sr. and Vickie Buckendorf, and my brother Matt for their support of this project. Also included are my kids, Nathan and Gwendolyn, and my lovely girlfriend, Sandi, for being patient and understanding while I was busy working.

I would also like to thank Marc Carlson at the University of Tulsa, Chris Wright at the Oklahoma City Air Logistics Center History Office, Jennifer Kolise at Camp Gruber, Keith Welch of American Legion Post 1, Natalie Pagano of Manhattan Construction, and fellow collectors Keith Myers, Dewey Wilson, and Kevin O'Keefe. Then, of course, there are the veterans themselves, my inspiration and constant source of hero worship, though they themselves are too humble to ever claim such things. Chief among them is my friend Sgt. Ray Amstutz, World War II veteran and lifelong Tulsan. I could not have done this book without any of them.

INTRODUCTION

The sun is setting on the "Greatest Generation," that twilight descending faster with each year. What remains of their legacy is up to the generations that succeed them, and it would be a tragedy for the accomplishments of these men and women to be forgotten. They were a different breed, a generation dominated by stark social contradictions, yet possessed of a noble quality that proved to be truly world-changing. They lived in a time of entrenched racism, segregation, and sexism, yet within that time, the seeds of change, equality, and advancement were already beginning to bear fruit.

This generation possessed an innate ability to rise up and succeed beyond even their own wildest expectations. From the 1930s and the depths of the Great Depression to the golden boom years of postwar expansion, a mere 15 years had passed. It took a massive government restructuring—in the form of the New Deal—to get the ball of recovery rolling, but it took the largest war in human history to bring that ball crashing into reality.

Tulsa is but one city that can boast tales of overcoming adversity and reaping the fruits of a hard-won victory. But what few realize is that Tulsa, and indeed all of Oklahoma, had a lot more at stake. Due to the Depression, we were far more impoverished than our cousins back east or the seemingly untouched beacon of hope that was California. If suffering through the economic crash was not bad enough, in 1934, Oklahoma also had the Dust Bowl to contend with. The vast exodus of Okies who took to the roads became a part of the American lexicon. To those who remained behind, there were challenges ahead—endless hard times that the New Deal only partially alleviated. For Tulsa, there was also lingering shame of the 1921 race riot, which all but destroyed the all-black neighborhoods of the Greenwood District on May 31st and June 1st of that year, with an estimated body count of over 300. This incident remained buried for decades, as both whites and blacks either purposefully ignored the event or spoke of it in quiet tones, and seldom in public.

War has a way of pushing old animosities aside as a community forgets its own differences and unites to take on a more encompassing threat. After the attack on Pearl Harbor, even the staunchest of isolationists could no longer justify the claim that America had no business in world affairs. Tulsa was in a unique position to take advantage of the opportunities brought on by wartime mobilization. After all, Tulsa was the "Oil Capital of the World" at one point. Tulsa fell in love with aviation during the 1920s, and not even the Depression quelled that passion. There was also a question of manpower; young adults—boys, in many cases—swelled the ranks of the military. Many came back as men, seasoned in experience if not in years, while many came back only as memories, as gold stars in windows and terse, tear-stained Western Union telegrams.

This book cannot hope to grasp the enormity of their involvement, sacrifices, and stunning successes. What it does is provide a brief snapshot, a window into the past designed to give the reader an opportunity to glimpse the city of Tulsa in a way that it will never be again.

V-E DAY
TULSA

Tulsans celebrated the end of the war and Victory in Europe (VE) Day with a ticker-tape parade and celebration throughout downtown. This is a view of 415 South Boston Avenue near the Atlas Life Building. (Courtesy of the Oklahoma Collection, Coll. No. 2006.012, Department of Special Collections and University Archives, McFarlin Library, University of Tulsa.)

One

THE DEPRESSION
AND THE ROADS TO
RECOVERY AND WAR

Following World War I, the economy in Tulsa remained relatively intact. Perhaps it was because of Tulsa's geographic location in the center of the nation or the area's abundance of natural resources, but Tulsa enjoyed extensive growth during the Roaring Twenties, although there was an economic downturn at its conclusion, including a loss of oil revenue.

Tulsa's potable water problems were finally solved with the building of the Spavinaw Dam, and an increased population meant residential and commercial development. By the mid-1920s, Tulsa boasted a number of buildings standing 10 to 20 stories high. Both Curtis-Southwest Airplane Company and Spartan Aircraft Company brought business to the city, and a 1928 resurgence in oil production in Eastern Oklahoma seemed to herald a return to the prosperity of the days when big money tycoons like Tate Brady, Thomas Gilcrease, and Frank Phillips helped put the city on the map. The 1929 stock market crash tipped a falling row of dominoes that put the brakes on the good times.

The Great Depression hit the state of Oklahoma and Tulsa quite hard. One out of every four Americans was out of work, and a vast army of hundreds of thousands of the dispossessed, many of them homeless teenagers, illegally rode the rails and subsisted in hobo jungles. In Tulsa, 7,000 people were out of work, and soup lines stretched across the Eleventh Street Bridge. Outlaws like Pretty Boy Floyd, Machine Gun Kelly, and Clyde Barrow and Bonnie Parker crisscrossed the state during their violent crime sprees. Some people called them folk heroes, others said they were murderers.

The ravages of the Dust Bowl, in which vicious high-speed winds ripped up the soil and created a wall of airborne particles that turned the very sky itself a dusky brown, sent the already hurting agricultural economy spiraling downward. Thousands took to the roads in caravans of desperation, most following rumors of farm work waiting in California. Many never found it, with the farms and orchards already full of those who got there first.

The divide between monopolies and unionization was stark, and with the "Roosevelt Recession" of Pres. Franklin D. Roosevelt's second term, large corporations were still looked upon with distrust. For Tulsa, that was defined by the Mid-Continent Refinery strike of 1938, which saw riots that culminated in the National Guard being called out to restore order. The strike remained in arbitration until 1940. The nation was in a populist mood, and Roosevelt was a populist president. During Roosevelt's first term, the government offered immediate relief and recovery in the form of organizations like the Works Progress Administration (WPA), the National Recovery Administration, and the Civilian Conservation Corps (CCC), giving people hope and the impetus to rebuild. His second term, however, was marked with an increasingly militant atmosphere surrounding the unions, violent strikes, perpetually low wages, and still rampant unemployment. In Tulsa, successes like the WPA-funded construction of Daniel Webster and Will Rogers High Schools in 1938 offered signs that recovery was evident but by no means complete. On some fronts, the end of the decade showed little difference from its beginning.

Worldwide responses to the Depression were far different and ultimately damaging. Japan's landgrabs in China and atrocities like the Nanking Massacre soured relations between that country and the United States; economic sanctions against Japan only deepened this divide. Adolf Hitler's programs rebuilt the German economy and put people back to work, but at the cost of severe racial and ethnic oppression. Jim Crow segregation was bad in the United States, but the Racial Purity Laws were far worse, stripping German Jews of every legal protection. The Holocaust had not yet begun, but the groundwork was being laid for it.

President Roosevelt realized the threats posed by both belligerent powers. Regardless of the isolationist element, confrontation seemed to be inevitable. Shifting to a wartime economy offered a twofold answer to the nation's economic crisis, and Tulsa, like many cities, helped to provide resources to meet the need. Oklahoma's governor during World War II, Leon "Red" Phillips, was no friend of President Roosevelt and wanted little to do with the New Deal or the military buildup. It was up to local community leaders to petition for federal defense contracts. Federal Housing Administration loans funded residential developments for the flood of defense workers that poured into Tulsa. These workers, many of them women, were desperately needed, as thousands of men had been put into uniform after the Selective Training and Service Act of 1940.

The oil industry charged to the forefront, along with aviation and the railroads, and by 1942, they were joined by nearly every conceivable business. Production shifted from consumer goods to military orders; after America's entry into the war in December 1941, output reached staggering heights, and Tulsa's contribution on all fronts proved significant.

Downtown Tulsa is pictured here as it appeared in the years prior to World War II. At the time, the largest buildings were the Philtower (left) and National Bank Building (right). Today, these 20-story buildings are dwarfed by modern structures like the Bank of Oklahoma (BOK) Tower. (Courtesy of the Oklahoma Collection, Coll. No. 2006.012, Department of Special Collections and University Archives, McFarlin Library, University of Tulsa.)

Thanks to Tulsa's love of aviation, numerous aerial photographs exist of the growing downtown area; this image dates back to 1931. (Author's collection.)

Tulsa's oil and industrial capacity is vividly demonstrated in this early-1930s photograph showing the Eleventh Street Bridge from the east bank of the Arkansas River. Smoke pours from funnels at the Conoco Oil Company and the industrial parks dotting the west banks of the river. (Courtesy of the Beryl Ford Collection/Rotary Club of Tulsa, Tulsa City-County Library and Tulsa Historical Society.)

The Twenty-first Street Bridge, which connected downtown with growing commercial and residential interests in Tulsa's West Side, was constructed in 1932 through funds raised in a citywide bond drive. The 21-span, open-spandrel arch bridge was heavily renovated in 1984. (Courtesy of the Oklahoma Collection, Coll. No. 2006.012, Department of Special Collections and University Archives, McFarlin Library, University of Tulsa.)

P-01-30

Many new construction projects in the 1930s, including this Manhattan Construction site, were at least partially subsidized, if not wholly funded, through New Deal agencies like the Works Progress Administration (WPA). Manhattan Construction later won several defense contracts during the war, building airfields, Army camps, and factories. (Courtesy of Manhattan Construction.)

Shown here is an electric trolley from the now-defunct Sand Springs line. Ever mindful of civic development, Tulsa oilman Charles Page, founder of the Tulsa suburb of Sand Springs, established a colony for widows and orphans in 1912. He constructed his own railway system to connect the community with greater Tulsa, thereby providing Tulsa's first mass transit system. The Sapulpa Union provided similar services. These lines were largely obsolete by the time America entered the war and were eventually phased out of service. (Courtesy of the Matt Buckendorf collection.)

The Sand Springs line began with two gasoline-powered railroad engines, which were quickly replaced by electric trolleys that operated between Tulsa and Sand Springs until 1955. Receipts from Page's trolley line went toward funding the home for widows and orphans. (Courtesy of the Matt Buckendorf collection.)

The Mincks Hotel, located at 403 South Cheyenne Avenue and also known as the Mincks-Adams Building, was erected in 1928 to capitalize on Tulsa's International Petroleum Exposition. It is a unique building that combines Baroque, Gothic, and Italian Renaissance architectural features. (Courtesy of the Oklahoma Collection, Coll. No. 2006.012, Department of Special Collections and University Archives, McFarlin Library, University of Tulsa.)

At 409 South Boston Avenue, from left are the Cosden, Atlas Life, and Philtower buildings. The Cosden was actually Tulsa's first skyscraper, a 15-story concrete reinforced structure built on the site of Tulsa's first schoolhouse, a Creek Nation Mission School. (Courtesy of the Oklahoma Collection, Coll. No. 2006.012, Department of Special Collections and University Archives, McFarlin Library, University of Tulsa.)

The Mayo Hotel, constructed in 1925 at 115 West Fifth Street, fell on hard times when the oil boom ended in the early 1980s. Having once hosted celebrities like Babe Ruth and Mae West, it sat derelict for two decades with all but the lower three floors gutted. It underwent renovations beginning in 2001 and has again become a major attraction of the city's downtown district. (Courtesy of the Oklahoma Collection, Coll. No. 2006.012, Department of Special Collections and University Archives, McFarlin Library, University of Tulsa.)

The Petroleum Building, erected in 1921 at 420 South Boulder Avenue next to the Mayo Hotel, was named for the numerous oil company offices it once contained. The building is most famous for housing the Mayo Brothers Furniture Company for over 50 years. (Courtesy of the Oklahoma Collection, Coll. No. 2006.012, Department of Special Collections and University Archives, McFarlin Library, University of Tulsa.)

At 1010 East Eighth Street, architect Frederick W. Kershner designed the building formerly known as the Tulsa Fire Alarm Building. Erected in 1934, it is an excellent example of Art Deco design. It is based on a Mayan temple, with intricate friezes depicting firefighters and related imagery. The Fire Alarm Building was a central connection for all of Tulsa's alarm systems, enabling firemen stationed there to alert the proper firehouses when emergencies occurred. It became derelict in 1984 but was refurbished and is now the local office for the American Lung Association. (Author's collection.)

Despite the Depression, Tulsans still enjoyed a festive atmosphere, as shown in this Christmas 1938 photograph of downtown. (Courtesy of Harvey Shell.)

The coastal cities of the United States learned the hard way to keep city lights extinguished for fear of providing a beacon for Axis submarines to home in on. As the war progressed and Axis bombings of the nation's heartland proved unlikely, blackout restrictions were relaxed, as demonstrated in this shot of the illuminated Philtower and National Bank buildings. Thanks to a central continental location, Tulsans were able to enjoy the lights and festivities of the holidays. (Courtesy of the Oklahoma Collection, Coll. No. 2006.012, Department of Special Collections and University Archives, McFarlin Library, University of Tulsa.)

This is an aerial view of downtown Tulsa, looking west, in 1945. (Courtesy of the Beryl Ford Collection/Rotary Club of Tulsa, Tulsa City-County Library and Tulsa Historical Society.)

The Texaco Refinery is shown in the 1930s in this photograph facing east toward downtown. The refinery, later purchased by Sinclair and now owned by the Holly Corporation, sits on the west bank of the Arkansas River, on Southwest Boulevard between Twenty-fifth and Thirty-sixth Streets. The north-south rail track belonged to the Midland Valley railway. (Courtesy of the Oklahoma Collection, Coll. No. 2006.012, Department of Special Collections and University Archives, McFarlin Library, University of Tulsa.)

The WPA funded the creation of Woodward Park and the Tulsa Rose Garden in 1934 through 1935. The rose garden features over 250 different varieties of roses and remains a popular attraction and wedding spot. (Author's collection.)

Woodward Park, at Twenty-first Street and Peoria Avenue, boasts 34 acres of botanical gardens, walking paths, an arboretum, and elaborate stonework laid by WPA workers using teams of horses and hand tools. (Author's collection.)

This late-1930s photograph offers an aerial view looking west toward the Tulsa Rose Garden and Woodward Park. The Twenty-first Street Bridge, which crosses the Arkansas River into West Tulsa, is visible at top left. (Courtesy of the Beryl Ford Collection/Rotary Club of Tulsa, Tulsa City-County Library and Tulsa Historical Society.)

Greenleaf State Park, outside Muskogee, was another major New Deal building project during the Depression era in Oklahoma. Close to Tulsa, it was a great natural getaway. (Courtesy of Camp Gruber.)

This image shows Greenleaf Lodge, the heart of Greenleaf State Park. The lake cabins, hiking trails, camping facilities, and other features were built in a joint effort by the WPA, the CCC, and, later, German POWs. (Courtesy of Camp Gruber.)

Historic Fort Gibson, originally established during the time of Indian Removal in the 1830s, was part of a network of military outposts dotting Indian Territory throughout the 19th century. By the 1930s, it was little more than a ruin. As shown here, the WPA completely reconstructed the fort and surrounding buildings in 1936. (Courtesy of Correy Twilley.)

The ruins of a Civilian Conservation Corps camp that serviced Northeastern Oklahoma, including the Tulsa area, during the 1930s are located outside of Bartlesville, Oklahoma. This is the fireplace from the camp's central meeting hall. (Author's collection.)

In Northeastern Oklahoma, the CCC was responsible for constructing most of the state's nature and hiking trails, as well as bridges and roads like this one alongside the Osage Hills Nature Preserve just north of Tulsa. (Author's collection.)

Pictured here are the ruins of a CCC storage building, where dynamite and blasting caps were stored during the camp's operation, near the Osage Hills Nature Preserve. The explosives were used for clearing boulders and obstructions. Critics of the CCC derided the organization as being militaristic in nature, but the discipline instilled into its recruits served them well when the war broke out. (Author's collection.)

Two

WINGS OVER TULSA

It is no surprise that the first aviation enthusiasts were rich. To fly, to take wing in the air, was a tremendous novelty to the Oklahoma oilmen of the early 20th century. Like the automobile before the invention of Henry Ford's revolutionary assembly-line system, airplanes were all custom-built, and only the wealthy could afford them prior to and just after World War I. Oilmen like William Skelly and Waite Phillips had their own planes and by and large used them as toys. Despite the use of fighter planes in World War I, the potential of aircraft had barely begun to be realized.

Numerous small airports dotted the city of Tulsa. McIntyre Airport once stood at the corner of Admiral Boulevard and Sheridan Road; farther south was Garland Airport at Fifty-first Street and Sheridan Road. Other airports included the North American Airlines Field and the W.F. Wilcox Field, the latter of which was also home to manufacturing company Collier Aircraft.

William Skelly's vision for aeronautics was far-reaching, and differed from those of many of his peers. Skelly founded Spartan Aircraft Company in 1928, the same year Tulsa opened its municipal airport. It still remains in operation today as the Spartan School of Aeronautics and is located on the same grounds. J. Paul Getty bought out Skelly's interest in the company in 1935, but Spartan's impressive manufacturing capabilities were already being utilized. Spartan began building open-cockpit trainers for the military, and before the United States officially entered World War II, its facilities were already being used to train U.S. Army Air Force pilot cadets and Royal Air Force cadets.

Tulsa's Municipal Airport bears no resemblance whatsoever to its sprawling modern successor, Tulsa International. When the municipal airport first opened to air traffic in July 1928, it had only two aircraft hangars. It soon saw visitations by aviation luminaries—such as Amelia Earhart, Charles and Anne Morrow Lindbergh, Frank Hawks, local sons like Wiley Post, and, perhaps most importantly, Jimmy Doolittle, who would go on to envision and command the famed carrier-launched B-25 raid over Tokyo in 1942. Tulsa Municipal became a hub for the delivery of airmail, with the first delivery run to Ponca City in 1929. In 1936, American Airlines expanded service to include Tulsa, and by the end of the war in 1945, the company established a permanent presence there. Other new facilities included Harvey Young Airport on 135th East Avenue, which opened in 1941 and also served as a training field. After the war, Harvey Young Airport remained the only privately owned general aviation airport in the Tulsa area.

The most enduring example of wartime aviation, however, was the Douglas Bomber plant, a mile-long behemoth that was a tremendous boon to both the national war effort and to Tulsa. In 1942, Douglas opened the huge facility at Sheridan Road and Apache Street near Tulsa Municipal Airport and began building and modifying bombers. Douglas was established in Santa Monica,

California, in 1921. A Douglas plane performed the first circumnavigation of the world by air in 1924, but this was surpassed by the company's development of the DC-3, the world's first large-scale air transport, better known by its military designation, the C-47 Skytrain, or *Dakota*. Douglas also ventured into a consortium with aviation giants Boeing and Vega to produce the B-17 bomber, the vaunted Flying Fortress of World War II.

Shortly after its founding, Douglas became a major contractor for the US Navy, expanding operations to include plants in Santa Monica, Long Beach, Chicago, and eventually Oklahoma. A plant was constructed in Midwest City, near Oklahoma City, and by 1942, Tulsa was home to a plant as well. The Tulsa bomber plant built Dauntless dive-bombers, Consolidated B-24 Liberator bombers, B-25 Mitchell medium-range bombers, and A-26 Invaders. At one time, Douglas plants boasted as many 160,000 employees countrywide. To say that Tulsa's economy thrived as a result of the Douglas plant is an understatement. Sadly, at the conclusion of the war, the Tulsa plant was downgraded due to a lack of government work orders, and Douglas trimmed its workforce by some 99,000 employees. However, American Airlines was quick to capitalize on this in December 1945 and took over the modification hangars formerly occupied by Douglas. These eventually became part of the world's largest air maintenance facilities and remain in operation today. Other parts of the bomber plant are now home to Spirit Aviation and the Tulsa Bus Plant. Rockwell Aviation operated there during the 1970s and 1980s, building components for the space shuttle program.

This is Tulsa Municipal Airport as it appeared in the 1930s. (Courtesy of the Beryl Ford Collection/Rotary Club of Tulsa, Tulsa City-County Library and Tulsa Historical Society.)

This statue stands at the entrance to the Tulsa International Airport in commemoration of the Army Air Force personnel that trained in Tulsa during the war. (Author's collection.)

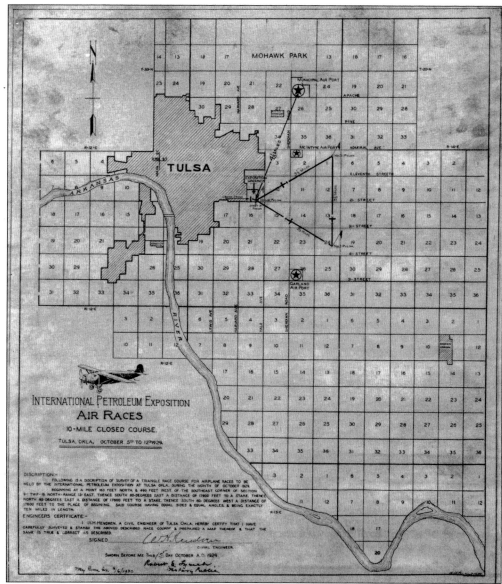

This 1929 poster from the International Petroleum Exposition demonstrates the ties between aviation and oil in the early 20th century. The 10-mile closed-course air race began at Tulsa's Exposition Grounds (currently the fairgrounds at Twenty-first Street and Yale Avenue), expanded into a triangular path that extended to the present-day location of Forty-first Street and Mingo Road, then on to Admiral Boulevard, and finally, returned to the exposition grounds. Note that though the grid work is laid out for the present-day city, the boundaries of Tulsa itself were confined to the shaded areas to the left of the exposition grounds in 1929. (Courtesy of the Matt Buckendorf collection.)

This is a c. 1941 aerial view of Spartan Aircraft Company. The company's first production model, the C-3 open-cockpit biplane, was designed in 1926 as a trainer for flight schools. By World War II, Spartan began production of the Zeus 8W for the military, a reconnaissance and training aircraft based on its high-end 7W model, which was envisioned by company founder William Skelly as a high-flying luxury toy for the wealthy. (Courtesy of the Beryl Ford Collection/Rotary Club of Tulsa, Tulsa City-County Library and Tulsa Historical Society.)

Virgil Fichter, shown here at Spartan, served as a flight instructor for Royal Air Force Pilot Cadets in No. 3 British Flying Training Squadron from September 1941 to September 1945. (Courtesy of Keith Welch.)

In this image, Virgil Fichter climbs into an AT-6 trainer. This was a typical plane used for pilot instruction. Many examples of these planes can be seen in the Tulsa skies today as they fly out of R.L. Jones Airport in nearby Jenks. (Courtesy of Keith Welch.)

Another trainer, the BT-19, is pictured here. Note the heavy leather and fleece flight suits worn by pilots. At high altitudes, hypothermia and oxygen deprivation were always issues. (Courtesy of Keith Welch.)

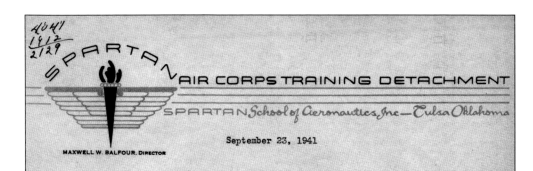

SPARTAN AIR CORPS TRAINING DETACHMENT

SPARTAN School of Aeronautics, Inc — Tulsa Oklahoma

September 23, 1941

MAXWELL W. BALFOUR, Director

Mr. Virgil C. Fitcher
Mexico, Missouri (821 East Monroe)

Dear Mr. Fitcher:

Confirming our telephone conversation of Monday, I will be expecting you on Thursday, September 25, at Miami, Oklahoma. Report there to Mr. A.J. Ming for interview and flight check. You will find him at the airport which has been taken over by a division of Spartan School now training British subjects. Briefly, employment conditions in our advanced training program are as follows:

We are under contract with the British Government for primary and advanced training of military personnel which is assigned to us at the rate of fifty every five weeks. This training is entirely under our supervision and done entirely by our employees. Instructors are consequently employed strictly as civilians.

Before we can employ any candidate, it is necessary, of course, that we interview him to determine if he has the proper personality and qualifications for this type of work. It is also essential that he submit to a flight check so that we can judge his flying ability and his possibilities as an instructor. This flight check is not severe; it is given principally to determine if the candidate is basically a sound pilot and knows how to impart instruction.

Acceptable candidates are placed in our military instructors school and given a course of instruction ranging from twenty-five to thirty-five hours. His work is closely supervised by special instructors whose efforts are directed towards helping him meet our required standard. The candidate is given every opportunity to correct his defects and make good. This course is given entirely at our expense. This instruction is given in the BT-13A Vultee, 450 H.P., or the AT-6A North American, 550 H.P. The training specializes in various types of desired maneuvers, formation, instrument and night flying.

During this course of instruction the prospect is not on an employment status. He is, however, given an allowance of $100.00 per month to help him defray his expenses.

Immediately upon completion of the course, he is placed on employment status with pay beginning at $300.00 per month. At the end of three months,

This correspondence lays out the purpose and duties of Spartan School of Aeronautics as it took on a training role for pilot cadets. Note the wartime name change to "Spartan Air Corps Training Detachment." (Courtesy of Keith Welch.)

if he is doing average work or better, he is granted an increase to $325.00 per month. If his progress is slow but he is making an honest effort, we give him further opportunity to improve, and at any time in the next three months when we consider that he has reached the proper quality of performance, we grant his increase to $325.00 per month.

At the end of twelve months service, an increase to $350.00 is given, at the end of eighteen months to $375.00, and at the end of two years to $400. Flight Commanders are paid $25.00 per month in addition to base pay, and Class Commanders, $50.00.

While we cannot make any promises regarding the permanency of this work and consequently do not give any permanent contracts, we do have every reason to believe that this program will go on indefinitely, and we do have very good reason to believe it will be permanent.

Working conditions are agreeable. Very rarely do any of our instructors leave our service. Normally, we work five days a week, never more than eight hours a day. A one week rest period is usually given at the end of every ten weeks. No deductions are made from pay for ordinary sickness or occasional days off for personal reasons.

We believe that this is the most interesting type of instruction work a man could engage in. From this work he can go to almost any type of flying. While we do not bind anyone with a contract since we feel that pilot contracts are useless, we do expect a gentleman's agreement to remain with us a minimum of one year to compensate us for the expensive training we give the candidate.

I am enclosing an application form and questionnaire which I would like to have you fill out and return to me at once, in order that I may have them by Thursday morning if possible. Enclose with these a recent clear photograph of yourself, if you have one available.

I am counting on seeing you Thursday unless circumstances alter your plans, in which case I would like to have you let me know by Western Union.

Sincerely yours,

SPARTAN SCHOOL OF AERONAUTICS

Maxwell W. Balfour

1-2
2 encl.

This continues the correspondence from the previous page. It is interesting to note that though the work of training pilot cadets is described as ongoing and indefinite, the program was shut down within days of the war ending. (Courtesy of Keith Welch.)

Accidents were common, and some pilot cadets were killed in the course of training. Royal Air Force pilot cadets who lost their lives in Oklahoma during the war remain interred at the former Spartan Aircraft Company training field in Miami, Oklahoma. (Courtesy of the Beryl Ford Collection/Rotary Club of Tulsa, Tulsa City-County Library and Tulsa Historical Society.)

This US Army Air Force B-24 crew in training was luckier than many. When forced to make an emergency landing, they set down on the Spartan runway, which was not built to withstand heavy bomber planes. The plane tore up the runway upon landing, but thankfully, the crew walked away unhurt. (Courtesy of Keith Welch.)

This autographed photograph shows a group of US Army Air Force pilot cadets who underwent training at Spartan. Facilities for housing and training were spread around the Tulsa area. Airfields and barracks were also located at Hatbox Field in Muskogee, as well as in Miami, Oklahoma. (Courtesy of Keith Welch.)

This image depicts Royal Air Force Pilot Cadets, British personnel brought to Tulsa to train as fighter pilots before heading back overseas. Many of the Brits who trained here retained fond memories of their time in Oklahoma; ties remain strong to this day for the survivors. (Courtesy of Keith Welch.)

This was the barracks that housed British pilot cadets at Spartan's training facility in Miami, Oklahoma. Joint Anglo-American cooperation maintains the graves of pilot cadets who died during training and remain interred here. (Courtesy of Keith Welch.)

While this is dated 1949, it is identical to wartime certificates—comedic mementos awarded to pilot cadets upon graduation from flight school. They remain prized collector's pieces. (Courtesy of Keith Welch.)

These instructor flight log pages, dated February 1943, show the progress of British pilot cadets as they trained on AT-6 *Texan* aircraft at Spartan. (Courtesy of Keith Welch.)

The right-hand columns in the flight log indicate trainer remarks on individual maneuvers performed by the cadets, weather conditions, and overall performance. (Courtesy of Keith Welch.)

THIS PAGE BEGINS ON *Aug 11, 1945* AND ENDS ON *Sept 6, 1945* NAME OF AIRLINE #3 B.F.T.S.									
DATE 1945	FLIGHT NUMBER	FROM	TO	AIRCRAFT MAKE AND MODEL	AIRCRAFT CERTIFICATE MARK	MILES FLOWN	DURATION OF FLIGHT	CLASS 0 TO 300	CLASS 300 TO 825
Aug 11	1	Miami Okla	Miami Okla	NORTH-AMERICAN AT-6	Army	✓	40		40
Aug 14	1	Miami Okla	Local	FAIRCHILD PT-19	Army	✓	1 00		1 00
Aug 17	1	Miami Okla	Local	PT-19	Army	✓	1 10		1 10
Aug 18	1	Miami Okla	Local	N.A. AT-6	Army	✓	20		20
Aug 21	1	Miami Okla	Local	N.A.-AT-6	Army	✓	1 00		1 00
Aug 22	1	Miami Okla	Local	N.A.-AT-6	Army	✓	40		40
Aug 34	1	Miami Okla	Local	N.A.-AT-6	Army	✓	45		45
Aug 30	1	Miami Okla	Local	N.A.-AT-6	Army	✓	35		35
Sept 2	2	Miami Okla	Local	N.A. AT-6	Army	✓	1 30		1 30
Sept 3	5	Miami Okla	Local	N.A. AT-6	Army	✓	1 30		1 30
Sept 6	1	Miami Okla	Local	N.A. AT-6	Army	✓	1 00		1 00

End of Flying for Spartan School of Aeronautics
At Miami Okla, #3. B.F.T.S. A.A.F.C.C.F.S. #2556

IF YOU WISH TO CERTIFY EACH PAGE USE THIS SPACE			
CERTIFIED CORRECT_____	TOTALS FOR THIS PAGE ONLY	10 10	10 10
ATTESTED BY_____	TOTALS FORWARD FROM PRECEDING PAGE	6053 40 4438 48	1595 16
	GRAND TOTALS FORWARD TO NEXT PAGE	6063 50 4438 48	1605 26

Pictured here is Virgil Fichter's final wartime flight log entry. No. 3 British Flight Training Squadron officially ended operations upon the cessation of hostilities in September 1945. (Courtesy of Keith Welch.)

This is the dedication ceremony for the Tulsa Douglas bomber plant in 1942. Among others, the company produced A-26 medium-range bombers and Dauntless dive-bombers, as well as modifying and refurbishing thousands of B-24s, B-25s, and, pictured above, B-17 Flying Fortresses. The B-17 was a flying arsenal, with machine guns at the nose and tail, two ball turrets located on the top of the plane and below it—centered right behind the cockpit—and two at the waist. The B-17 carried a load capacity of 8,000 pounds of explosives, and it is estimated that B-17s dropped more than 640,000 tons of bombs throughout the war. (Courtesy of the Beryl Ford Collection/Rotary Club of Tulsa, Tulsa City-County Library and Tulsa Historical Society.)

The Douglas bomber plants at both Tulsa and Midwest City cranked out thousands of aircraft for the war effort. While its roots go back to 1921, the Douglas Aircraft Company is better known for its production of the DC-3 *Dakota* or its military variation, the C-47 Skytrain. The C-47 was a reliable workhorse, famously remembered for transporting paratroopers into Normandy and Holland, but it did so much more. It sustained the supply lines of the China-Burma-India Theater, with Air Transport Command pilots flying over the hump of the Himalayas, and was instrumental in ferrying equipment and wounded troops away from battlefronts to rear-area hospitals in all theaters of operations. It was an all-purpose aircraft that served the Air Transport Command and Naval Air Transport Service well, and in many ways was just as important to winning the war as the bombers and fighter planes built alongside them. (Courtesy of Oklahoma City Air Logistics Center History Office.)

A B-25 bomber rolls out of the production hangar at the Douglas Bomber plant. (Courtesy of Oklahoma City Air Logistics Center History Office.)

From 1942 to 1945, Douglas plants, such as those that operated in Tulsa and Midwest City, produced at least 16 percent of all the aircraft built during World War II—nearly 29,385 planes. (Courtesy of Oklahoma City Air Logistics Center History Office.)

The Douglas plant was a veritable beehive of activity that operated for 24 hours a day. Pictured here are overhead gantry cranes and stamping machines for creating aircraft components. (Courtesy of Oklahoma City Air Logistics Center History Office.)

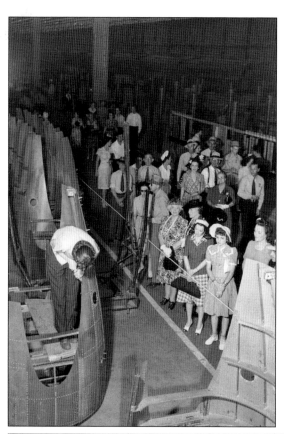

Here, a Rosie the Riveter bomber plant worker applies her craft to the aluminum engine cowling of an aircraft for a crowd of public spectators. (Courtesy of Oklahoma City Air Logistics Center History Office.)

The bomber plants at Tulsa and Midwest City were more than just sprawling industrial complexes. As this photograph of the offices demonstrates, running the business of a bomber facility took as much administrative staff as it did welders and riveters. (Courtesy of Oklahoma City Air Logistics Center History Office.)

Here, plant workers construct the tail sections for bomber aircraft. (Courtesy of Oklahoma City Air Logistics Center History Office.)

In this photograph, several Rosies and their male counterparts work on the nose section of a C-47 transport. (Courtesy of Oklahoma City Air Logistics Center History Office.)

This B-25 bomber, the *Tulsa Tuesday Forum*, was one of thousands modified at the Tulsa Douglas plant. Local civic groups and private clubs around town raised money through bond drives and earned the honor of having a bomber named after their organizations. The *T-Town Wolfess* was named after a baseball club, while the *Tulsa Vader* got its name from a local book club. The B-25 has an interesting roundabout historical connection with Tulsa. Prior to the war, Tulsa's Municipal Airport was visited by Lt. Col. Jimmy Doolittle, a longtime controversial proponent of strategic bombing who led a now-famous bombing raid over Tokyo in April 1942, flying B-25 bombers from the decks of the USS *Hornet* aircraft carrier. (Courtesy of the Beryl Ford Collection/Rotary Club of Tulsa, Tulsa City-County Library and Tulsa Historical Society.)

Pictured here is the *Tulsamerican*, the last B-24 bomber produced at the Tulsa bomber plant. It was lost on a bombing mission off the coast of Croatia, in the Adriatic Sea, on December 17, 1944. A dive team discovered its wreck at a 40-meter depth off Vis Island in March 2010. (Courtesy of the Beryl Ford Collection/Rotary Club of Tulsa, Tulsa City-County Library and Tulsa Historical Society.)

Three

GREASING THE WHEELS OF WAR

Oklahoma had two principal economic claims to fame in the early 20th century: petroleum and agriculture. When it came to Tulsa, however, the only business that truly mattered was the former of the two. The city's first oil well was discovered in West Tulsa's Red Fork community in 1901 but was quickly superseded by the enormous Glen Pool four years later, permanently wedding Tulsa to the oil business. The Glen Pool was so rich and produced so much oil that, at first, it couldn't be contained. Before the construction of tanks and pipelines, the oil had to be pumped into hastily built earthen pits. The Glen Pool produced up to 7,000 barrels a day, and lucrative contracts with the Frisco Railway soon granted rights-of-way straight to the oil fields for transport. Soon, a plethora of oil companies established roots in and around Tulsa, though city ordinances prevented drilling within the actual city limits. The companies included Gypsy, Phillips, Sunray, Kaiser-Francis, Skelly, and others. There was so much oil that it caused a glut in the market, as supply overrode demand in the early years of the Depression, causing oil prices to fall as low as 10¢ a barrel at one point. However, tying itself so intimately to one industry caused problems for Tulsa when it came to bad economic times.

Diversifying and expanding the economic base was an ongoing concern, but because of the Depression, little could be done about it. Shortly before the war began, 41 new oil fields were discovered in the state, and if it was good for the oil business, it was good for Oklahoma. Things took a dramatic turn when Gov. Red Phillips was voted out of office in 1942 and replaced by Robert S. Kerr, who had the background as an oilman to mend fences with the Roosevelt administration and secure tremendous amounts of funding for the state, converting its oil production for defense purposes. Business rebounded as a result. Consumer goods, while eventually rationed as the greater bulk became allocated to the military, were more plentiful than at the height of the Depression. More importantly, people were finally beginning to gain jobs, meaning that they could afford the goods. The manufacture of industrial products, especially for petroleum-related uses, caused vast new markets to open up for Tulsa companies. As a result of this adaptability, Tulsa became one of the state's focal points for wartime industrial growth.

Along with the increase in money came additional government contracts and the need for increased speed of production. Tulsa's industries rose to the challenge. Manhattan Construction Company set to work building hangars for the aircraft plants and barracks to house soldiers and defense contractors, earning huge defense contracts in the process. The pace of wartime production was frantic, and Manhattan proved more than capable, managing to build the sprawling Camp Gruber complex outside of Muskogee in only four months in 1942. Almost every industrial business in Tulsa shifted and adapted focus to meet wartime demand in a show of unity that would be unheard of in today's markets.

Even amidst the flurry of wartime production and activity, Tulsa businesses found time to indulge in cooperative ventures that aided the community with only peripheral connections to military-related work orders, such as the organization of Tulsa businesses to form the Co-Operative Club of Tulsa. The Co-Operative Club included a variety of average, independent businesses not connected with the oil and railroad conglomerates, such as Shaw Brothers Motor Company, Palace Clothiers, the Stephenson-Browne Lumber Company, and some names still familiar to Tulsans today, like Boston Cleaners and Dryers. Working in conjunction with the Tulsa Chamber of Commerce, the Co-Operative Club operated under the motto, "Make Life Worthwhile." The club often pooled money to reward community service volunteers for their efforts, sending entire troops of Girl Scouts to summer camp in recognition of their work organizing scrap-metal drives and volunteering for the American Red Cross and the Office of Civil Defense.

One Tulsa company, Perrault Brothers, manufactured pipeline equipment and related supplies for oil companies during and following the war. (Courtesy of the Matt Buckendorf collection.)

For decades, Tulsa's Exposition Center hosted an annual Oil Show celebrating the city's oil wealth and boasting of its industrial capacity. The Diamond Chain & Manufacturing Company exhibit from the 1940 show is pictured here. (Courtesy of the Beryl Ford Collection/Rotary Club of Tulsa, Tulsa City-County Library and Tulsa Historical Society.)

Here, engineers and designers for Perrault Brothers display a machine designed to encircle pipelines and clean the outside diameter in preparation for coating and wrapping. (Courtesy of the Matt Buckendorf collection.)

This view demonstrates how the cleaner was attached to the pipeline. It was self-propelled, riding atop the pipeline as wire brushes rotated about the outside of the pipe. (Courtesy of the Matt Buckendorf collection.)

Reaching the oil through drilling and capping the well were only the beginning steps. Pipelines had to be constructed to transport the raw crude oil, and Tulsa companies were among the front-runners in providing the necessary components. Individual pipeline parts came from places like Tennessee, Ohio, and Tulsa. This connection and cooperation of related industries made the "Arsenal of Democracy" run that much smoother. (Courtesy of the Matt Buckendorf collection.)

M.J. Crose Manufacturing, another Tulsa-based company, built pipeline-wrapping machines, such as this one, that inhibited corrosion on buried pipelines. (Courtesy of the Matt Buckendorf collection.)

Here, pipelines are coated with tar to prevent corrosion prior to being buried. Once a pipeline was cleaned and wrapped, the coating machine would lay down a layer of tar. (Courtesy of the Matt Buckendorf collection.)

This is another example of wrapping a pipeline. Note the trench to the lower left of the pipe. After wrapping and coating, the pipe will be lowered into the trench and buried. (Courtesy of the Matt Buckendorf collection.)

Side-boom tractors supported the pipe and towed the trailers filled with tar and wrapping material. Several Tulsa companies took standard Caterpillar and International tractors and fabricated side-boom attachments for oil field and pipeline use. (Courtesy of the Matt Buckendorf collection.)

Workers use a welding torch to cut out a section of pipe that failed a pressure test. (Courtesy of the Matt Buckendorf collection.)

Workers align sections of pipe. The block and tackle attached to the side-boom tractor at left was just one component manufactured by Tulsa companies that is still utilized today. (Courtesy of the Matt Buckendorf collection.)

Welders bevel a part of a pipe in preparation for welding an adjoining section to it. (Courtesy of the Matt Buckendorf collection.)

This is a crane built by the Unit Rig Company in Tulsa. Here, workers are predrilling prior to construction of a caisson. Similar cranes were utilized by the military for loading and unloading equipment onto and off of transport vessels. (Courtesy of the Matt Buckendorf collection.)

The oil business and the railroads have gone hand in hand in Tulsa since the Glen Pool was discovered in 1905. During the war, railroads that ran through Oklahoma, like the Frisco and Katy lines, hauled oil from fields and refineries to military bases and shipyards across the country; they were the lifelines of the war effort. But even then, they were used for so much more, such as transporting food, troops, and war material. (Author's collection.)

The Tulsa-Sapulpa Union (TSU) Railway connected Tulsa, Sapulpa, Glenpool, and Keifer and was originally an electric streetcar line dating back to 1907, the beginning of the oil boom. With the advent of the automobile, the trolley service eventually ended, but the line still serves industries, hauling freight back and forth between each city to this day. (Author's collection.)

The *Meteor* was a passenger train operated by the St. Louis–San Francisco Railway that ran an overnight service from Oklahoma City to St. Louis via Tulsa. No. 4500 was built during the war and was one of three (out of 25) Northern Class Baldwin 4-8-4 locomotives used on the *Meteor* line. It served to transport troops and civilian passengers. Its sister engine, the 4501, pulled Pres. Harry S. Truman on a whistle-stop tour shortly after the war concluded. The 4500 now sits on permanent display at the Route 66 Station Park in West Tulsa. (Author's collection.)

Troops traveling through Tulsa had roundabout methods for reaching their destinations. Leaving Tulsa by the Frisco line had a direct route to Fort Sill, but those traveling to nearby Camp Gruber, such as the troops shown above, traveled along either the Katy, Frisco, or Midland Valley lines to Muskogee, then connected to the Missouri Pacific at OK Junction for the final leg to Gruber. (Courtesy of Camp Gruber.)

Though rendered obsolete with the advent of the diesel locomotive, old workhorses like this 440 locomotive were put back into service for the duration of the war. (Courtesy of Camp Gruber.)

Oilman Frank Phillips oversees a scrap drive that involved collecting rubber from old tires and shoe heels for the war effort. (Courtesy of the Woolaroc Museum collection.)

Zebco, a long-standing Tulsa business known for manufacturing fishing reels, started in 1932 as the Zero Hour Bomb Company, which produced time bombs for fracturing oil well formations. Before the war, it was a struggling business in danger of going under. (Courtesy of Zebco.)

Tulsa-based Manhattan Construction was awarded several government contracts during the War, most notably the building of the Douglas Bomber Plant, Camp Gruber, and several other military bases across the country. (Courtesy of Manhattan Construction.)

Manhattan Construction finished the building of Camp Gruber, part of which is pictured at the top of the page, in a mere four months in 1942. In order to stay on schedule, Manhattan erected roughly one building per hour, totaling some 1,731 buildings. (Courtesy of Camp Gruber/National Archives.)

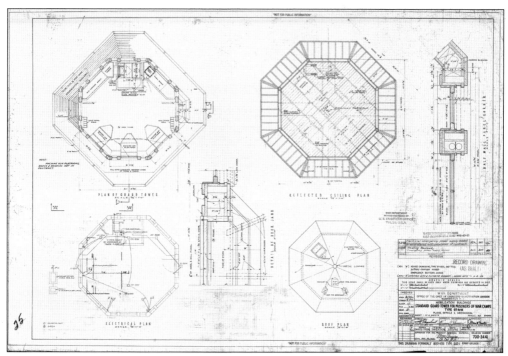

These are the blueprints for guard towers at Camp Gruber's prisoner-of-war facility built by Manhattan Construction. (Courtesy of Camp Gruber.)

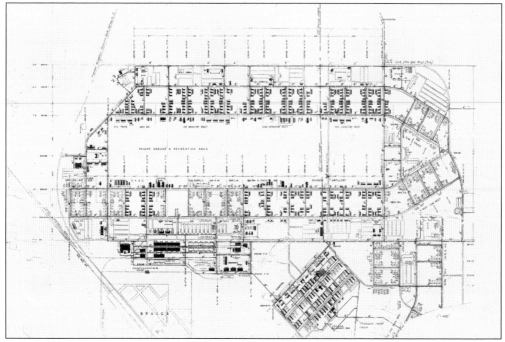

Pictured are blueprints for the entire cantonment of Camp Gruber, demonstrating the massive scale of the project taken on by Manhattan Construction when they secured the building contract. (Courtesy of Camp Gruber.)

The Oklahoma Tire and Supply retail chain began as the Oklahoma Salvage and Supply Company in the 1920s, and is far better known to Tulsans by its acronym, OTASCO. After opening in Okmulgee, the company moved its corporate offices to Tulsa in 1925. It was one of the few Tulsa companies that expanded during the Depression, having 34 stores open in 1936. By 1943, midway through the war, the company had more than 83 stores spread across four states. By the mid-1960s, there were over 450 stores across a dozen states. The company reached its zenith in the late 1980s and retains only a miniscule shadow of its former glory. (Courtesy of the Oklahoma Collection, Coll. No. 2006.012, Department of Special Collections and University Archives, McFarlin Library, University of Tulsa.)

Originally founded in 1902 as the Tulsa Commerce Club, the Tulsa Metro Chamber of Commerce (depicted here in its postwar offices) has been acting to expand and improve business opportunities in the Tulsa area for over a century. Today, a compact exists between the Tulsa chamber and those of the surrounding suburbs of Broken Arrow, Jenks, Sapulpa, Sand Springs, and Owasso. (Courtesy of the Oklahoma Collection, Coll. No. 2006.012, Department of Special Collections and University Archives, McFarlin Library, University of Tulsa.)

Borden/Meadow Gold began as Borden Dairy of Oklahoma and was purchased by the Beatrice Creamery Company in 1926. It originally delivered milk in horse-drawn wagons that used blocks of ice to keep the milk cool. This neon sign at the corner of Eleventh Street and Lewis Avenue was a familiar sight in Tulsa for decades before it was moved to its current location at Eleventh Street and Peoria Avenue. The company is now located downtown at 215 North Denver Street. (Author's collection.)

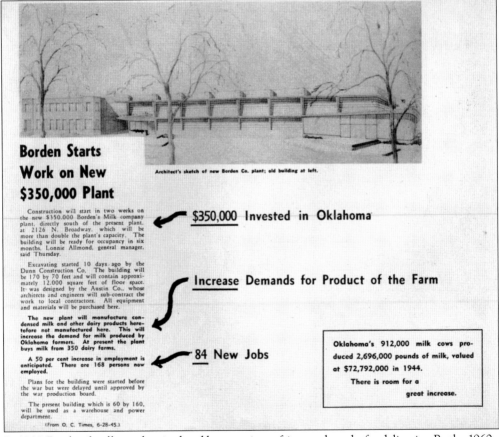

Architect's sketch of new Borden Co. plant; old building at left.

Borden Starts Work on New $350,000 Plant

Construction will start in two weeks on the new $350,000 Borden's Milk company plant, directly south of the present plant, at 2126 N. Broadway, which will be more than double the plant's capacity. The building will be ready for occupancy in six months, Lonnie Allmond, general manager, said Thursday.

Excavating started 10 days ago by the Dunn Construction Co. The building will be 170 by 70 feet and will contain approximately 12,000 square feet of floor space. It was designed by the Austin Co., whose architects and engineers will sub-contract the work to local contractors. All equipment and materials will be purchased here.

The new plant will manufacture condensed milk and other dairy products heretofore not manufactured here. This will increase the demand for milk produced by Oklahoma farmers. At present the plant buys milk from 350 dairy farms.

A 50 per cent increase in employment is anticipated. There are 168 persons now employed.

Plans for the building were started before the war but were delayed until approved by the war production board.

The present building which is 60 by 160, will be used as a warehouse and power department.

(From O. C. Times, 6-28-45.)

$350,000 Invested in Oklahoma

Increase Demands for Product of the Farm

84 New Jobs

> Oklahoma's 912,000 milk cows produced 2,696,000 pounds of milk, valued at $72,792,000 in 1944.
>
> There is room for a great increase.

In 1944, Borden finally modernized and began using refrigerated trucks for deliveries. By the 1960s, the company had over 150 home delivery routes. (Courtesy of the Oklahoma Collection, Coll. No. 2006.012, Department of Special Collections and University Archives, McFarlin Library, University of Tulsa.)

There were the exceptions to the wartime rule, like The Dawson Towel Company, which was located at 217 North Nogales Avenue. Companies that provided everyday staples basically continued business as usual, despite the war. Perhaps they felt the pinch of gasoline rationing but otherwise provided services without interruption. (Courtesy of Harvey Shell.)

Some now-defunct businesses live on as beloved architectural curiosities, such as this former Gulf Oil service station at Second Street and Elgin Avenue. It is hard to believe that such an elegant building (with a distinctive blue dome) served as a gas station when it was originally constructed in 1924. It now serves as the heart of downtown Tulsa's "Blue Dome" entertainment district. (Author's collection.)

Four

NIGHTSPOTS AND ENTERTAINMENT

Soldiers, sailors, and marines on leave, along with bond drive organizers, had a number of venues to choose from when it came to Tulsa nightlife. The West Side's Crystal City doubled as a dance hall with its Casa Loma Ballroom and as an amusement park. Downtown on South Main Street was the St. Moritz, but rumors circulated that it either catered to a seedy clientele or was a haven for Tulsa's then-closeted gay community. Of course, every nightspot was at least a little dangerous, considering that Oklahoma remained a dry state despite the repeal of Prohibition in 1933. The bootleggers of the gangster era maintained a healthy business in Tulsa, clandestinely delivering illegal booze across the city—or even delivering it to an individual's doorstep for $5 a bottle. Bootleggers even printed business cards with a price list for customer convenience.

Tulsa was known as one of the wettest places in the otherwise dry state. It is estimated that there were at least 200 illegal speakeasies within walking distance of downtown, and the consumption and distribution of alcohol within city limits was known for decades as "liquor by the wink." Even law enforcement officials were not immune to breaking the unpopular law; several police officers would regularly confiscate and dispose of seized alcohol, sometimes handing it over to political officials for consumption instead of destroying it. Oklahoma was one of the last states in the union to repeal Prohibition, eventually overturning it in 1959—by which time hardly anyone followed the law.

More accessible to the general public was the Buck Horn at Admiral Boulevard and Yale Avenue, which was an unusual drive-in with an open stage. The Blue Moon, which featured an open-air dance floor, was located at Fifty-sixth Street North and Cincinnati Avenue and is often remembered by patrons as a beautiful and romantic venue during the spring and summer months. Tulsans also flocked to theaters like the Ritz, the Orpheum, and the Majestic.

The most enduring venues were the larger halls and indoor stadiums (which often hosted big recording artists like the Glenn Miller Orchestra and Duke Ellington) that included the Akdar Shrine Temple and the Coliseum. Those still in operation include the former Tulsa Convention Hall (now known as the Brady Theater), the Mayo Hotel, and Cain's Ballroom. Tulsans who eschewed the nightlife sought out the solace of nature at beautiful venues like Woodward Park and the Tulsa Rose Garden or went sailing on Lake Yahola, just east of town. Others flocked to the Philbrook Museum of Art donated to the city by Tulsa oilman Waite Phillips.

Radio had proven a viable source for entertainment and news, which was advantageous when wartime rationing restricted the production of newsprint, leaving radio the most available resource for advertisers and the announcement of current events. The Federal Communications Commission (FCC) did not take over any stations during the war, but the Office of Censorship enforced regulations that prohibited broadcasting news that could be deemed sensitive, such as troop movements and manufacturing. The restrictions even included weather forecasts. Anything that could arguably be useful to a fifth columnist or Axis sympathizer was off-limits. Most people in Tulsa tuned in for the music, and while multiple local stations dotted the airwaves during the 1940s, the two leaders were KVOO and WKY. WKY imitated the broadcasting styles of East Coast radio stations, but KVOO was different, offering a sound that was distinctly Oklahoman. In the 1920s, listeners tuned in to hear acts like Otto Gray and his Oklahoma Cowboy Band, which went on to achieve more notoriety back east than the group ever did at home. In the 1940s, listeners were tuning in to hear Patti Page and the yodeling cowboy, Gene Autry.

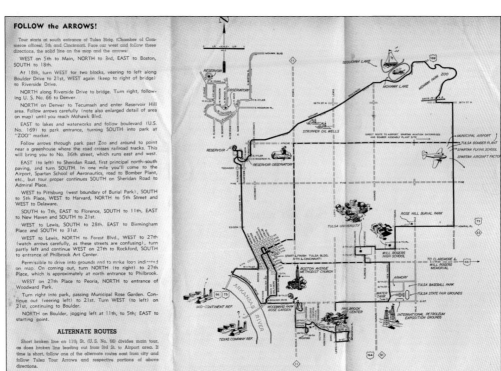

This is a Tulsa Chamber of Commerce tourism brochure from the 1940s that shows all of Tulsa's attractions. Note that the city limits at the time did not extend past Sheridan Road to the east and Thirty-first Street and Lewis Avenue to the south. (Courtesy of the Oklahoma Collection, Coll. No. 2006.012, Department of Special Collections and University Archives, McFarlin Library, University of Tulsa.)

Sailboaters enjoy the wind and waves of Lake Yahola, an artificial reservoir built in 1924. Lake Yahola is an integral part of Tulsa's water supply and is still a boating and fishing haven for many Tulsans. (Courtesy of the Beryl Ford Collection/Rotary Club of Tulsa, Tulsa City-County Library and Tulsa Historical Society.)

Tulsa's famous Akdar Shrine building originally stood at Fourth Street and Denver Avenue. The Akdar ("akdar" means "mightier or mightiest") Temple was originally established in 1922 and was the 125th Shriner temple erected in the United States. Considered an Art Deco architectural icon, the Akdar Temple served as a location for numerous bond drives and fundraising festivities during World War II. (Courtesy of the Beryl Ford Collection/Rotary Club of Tulsa, Tulsa City-County Library and Tulsa Historical Society.)

Tulsa's Coliseum, which was located between Fifth and Sixth Streets on Elgin Avenue, also served as a site for many wartime fundraisers. Originally built in 1929, the Coliseum was the home of the Tulsa Oilers hockey team. (Courtesy of the Oklahoma Collection, Coll. No. 2006.012, Department of Special Collections and University Archives, McFarlin Library, University of Tulsa.)

This was the official show program for the 1940 Ice Follies at the Coliseum, one of hundreds of such shows put on at the facility. Sadly, the beloved Coliseum burned to the ground after the war. In 1952, the Coliseum's demise was the first fire reported live by Tulsa's KOTV Channel 6. (Courtesy of the Beryl Ford Collection/Rotary Club of Tulsa, Tulsa City-County Library and Tulsa Historical Society.)

It was not just ice hockey and skaters; the Coliseum also frequently hosted Junior Chamber of Commerce fundraiser dinners, as well as high school proms and graduations. (Courtesy of the Beryl Ford Collection/Rotary Club of Tulsa, Tulsa City-County Library and Tulsa Historical Society.)

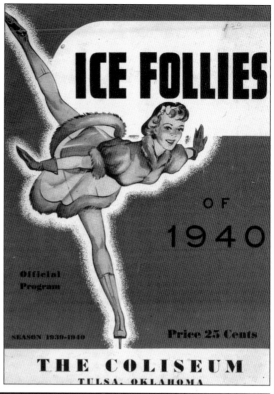

The Convention Hall (now known as Brady Theater) at 105 West Brady Street was opened in 1914 and has a rather tumultuous past. It has hosted performances by opera stars like Enrico Caruso and also served as a detention center for black refugees of Greenwood in the wake of the 1921 Tulsa race riot. During the war, the Convention Hall hosted several bond rallies and fundraisers. It remains a popular venue today. (Courtesy of the Oklahoma Collection, Coll. No. 2006.012, Department of Special Collections and University Archives, McFarlin Library, University of Tulsa.)

Cain's Ballroom was originally built in 1924 as a garage for the fleet of cars owned by oilman Tate Brady. In 1930, it was bought by Madison "Daddy" Cain and converted into a dance hall. Despite a sometimes rowdy past, it remains one of Tulsa's most iconic landmarks. (Author's collection.)

Here, Bob Wills and the Texas Playboys are onstage at Cain's Ballroom, also known as "The Home of Bob Wills." The band began as the "Light Crust Doughboys" in the early 1930s and migrated to Tulsa, where Cain's became their home. Despite a grueling touring schedule, the group seldom missed performing live broadcasts for Tulsa's KVOO radio station. Wartime conscription eventually depleted the band, prompting Wills to move to California in 1943, though he continued touring and often returned to Oklahoma after the war ended. (Courtesy of the Beryl Ford Collection/Rotary Club of Tulsa, Tulsa City-County Library and Tulsa Historical Society.)

GENE AUTRY

Gene Autry was a country-and-western icon who helped put Cain's on the map. Autry, who was working the night shift as a telegraph operator in Oklahoma when he was discovered by none other than Will Rogers, scored his first hit in 1932. Autry went on to act in more than 44 motion pictures and served in the Army Air Force from 1943 to 1945. (Author's collection.)

One of the most unique features of Cain's Ballroom is its "Wall of Fame," which contains giant portraits of the musical greats who played there from the 1930s through the 1950s. At left is Kay Starr, an Oklahoma gal described by Billie Holiday as "the only white woman who could sing the blues." (Author's collection.)

Jazz legend Count Basie first came to Tulsa in 1926, when he worked the vaudeville circuit as a young man. After being wowed by local jazz ensemble Walter Page Blue Devils, he fell in love with the big-band sound. Basie returned to Tulsa to play gigs at least twice—once in 1935 and again with his orchestra in 1943. (Courtesy of the Beryl Ford Collection/Rotary Club of Tulsa, Tulsa City-County Library and Tulsa Historical Society.)

The Ritz Theater was located at 410 South Main Street and hosted many War Bond Shows for the war effort. The Ritz closed in 1960 and was demolished in 1973. (Courtesy of the Beryl Ford Collection/Rotary Club of Tulsa, Tulsa City-County Library and Tulsa Historical Society.)

Wally's Pocket Menu

FROM THE DOWNTOWNER

What's Cookin' in Tulsa This week-end?

FRIDAY 12-4-42

SHOWS

ORPHEUM this week-end,"Thunder Birds",Gene Tierney,Preston Foster,John Sutton.Shows - 12:15 2:10 4:00 5:50 7:35 9:30

RITZ this weel-end,"White Cargo",Hedy Lamarr,Walter Pidgeon Shows - 11:55 1:30 3:30 5:35 7:25 9:30

MAJESTIC this week-end," For Me And My Gal",held over, Judy Garland,George Murphy,Gene Kelly.Shows - 11:35 1:25 3:25 5:30 7:30 9:30

RIALTO Thurs Fri Sat,"Laugh Your Blues Away,"Jinx Falkenburg, Bert Gordon (The Mad Russian) 2nd Feature,"Bandit Ranger", Cliff Edwards,Joan Barclay.

RIALTO Start Sun,"That Other Woman",Virginia Gilmore,James Ellison.

WRESTLING Coliseum Monday Night 8:30 PM Farmer Jones vs Speedy Larance.

DANCING

NIGHTLY The Music Box 4911 East Admiral Place 25¢ per person.Saturdays and holidays 45¢ per person inc. tax,Open all night.

SATURDAY NIGHT Casa Loma 9:30 'till 1:30 and Swingshifters dance 2:30 'till 5:30. Joe Linde and his Cafe Society Band. Both dances 75¢ per dancer inc. tax.

SKATING

ICE SKATING Coliseum Nightly except Monday 8 to 10:30 Afternoons except Mon.Tues. 2:30 to 5 Mornings Sat. and Sun.9:30 to 12

ROLLER SKATING Nightly Tulsa Fairgrounds Pavilion. Shuttle bus service from end of bus line,no extra charge.Special Ladies session Thurs.9:30 AM to 11:30 AM. Free instruction.

SPECIAL

Convention Hall every Sunday afternoon 2:30. Stage Show for Servicemen and their ladies - FREE. General public not invited. Cast and directed by "Hey Rube",Inc.

Pocket menus like this one were not only distributed in newspapers and advertising circulars but also enclosed in care packages to GIs overseas as morale boosters. A soldier missing home in some faraway locale might not have seen the logic in this. (Courtesy of the Oklahoma Collection, Coll. No. 2006.012, Department of Special Collections and University Archives, McFarlin Library, University of Tulsa.)

KVOO, a long-standing Tulsa radio station, began its broadcasting life in Bristow as KFRU in 1924. After being purchased by Tulsa oil magnate W.G. Skelly in 1925, the station moved to the location pictured here, atop Reservoir Hill in North Tulsa. It boasted a 25,000-watt capacity, and during the war, broadcasts of Bob Wills's shows reportedly could be heard as far away as California, even reaching Navy ships in the South Pacific on clear nights. (Courtesy of the Beryl Ford Collection/Rotary Club of Tulsa, Tulsa City-County Library and Tulsa Historical Society.)

The Spotlight Theater at 1381 Riverside Drive was originally built in the 1920s as a studio and recital hall for musician and teacher Patti Adams Shriner. During the war, it served as a speech and drama studio, and in 1953, it became the Spotlight Theater, famous for its renditions of *The Drunkard*. (Courtesy of the Oklahoma Collection, Coll. No. 2006.012, Department of Special Collections and University Archives, McFarlin Library, University of Tulsa.)

A comedy/variety show in the vaudeville tradition, the Hey Rubes Show traveled across the country offering free entertainment to the troops. In November 1942, the Hey Rubes Show played Tulsa's Convention Hall (now known as the Brady Theater). (Courtesy of the Beryl Ford Collection/Rotary Club of Tulsa, Tulsa City-County Library and Tulsa Historical Society.)

The bawdy antics of the Hey Rubes Show were thoroughly enjoyed by the troops. In addition to the dancing-girl acts, many of the performers in Hey Rubes were old-time vaudeville and minstrel show players, some of whom harkened back to the comedic styling of Al Jolson. (Courtesy of the Beryl Ford Collection/Rotary Club of Tulsa, Tulsa City-County Library and Tulsa Historical Society.)

Dancing at a USO club was a treat every serviceman looked forward to, no matter what city he was in. (Courtesy of the Keith Myers collection.)

The United Service Organization, which provides entertainment for the US Armed Forces, began working in conjunction with the Department of Defense in 1941. It was briefly disbanded in 1947 and revived for the Korean War. The USO is one World War II–inspired creation that continues in the modern era. To this day, Tulsa still hosts World War II–themed USO shows. (Author's collection.)

An official Army war show called *Tulsa Attacks!* was performed at Skelly Stadium on June 24, 1944. The show featured a football-field-sized mock-up of a Pacific island village, complete with faux palm trees and thatch huts, captured Japanese weapons and equipment, and a spectacular battle reenactment. A propaganda bond drive coup at the time, finding posters or tickets from this event today is a collector's dream. (Courtesy of the Beryl Ford Collection/Rotary Club of Tulsa, Tulsa City-County Library and Tulsa Historical Society.)

Pictured is an admission ticket to the *Tulsa Attacks!* war show hosted by the 8th Service Command at Skelly Stadium, which was located at Eleventh Street and Harvard Avenue. (Author's collection.)

OKLAHOMA • The Army Shows

★ The Eighth Service Command put on two four-day shows at Oklahoma City and Tulsa for the workers in the Douglas plants in both cities.

The shooting show simulated an attack on a Japanese atoll in the South Pacific, and untilized 1,000 crack combat-trained troops from nearby Camps Gruber, Crowder and Chaffee. Included in the $6,000,000 worth of equipment were 200 items of war, among them 30 ton medium tanks, tanks with 75 mm. guns, light tanks armed with 37 mm. cannon, tank destroyers, 37 mm. anti-tank guns, flame throwers as used at Tarawa, 50 calibre machine guns, bazookas and land mines.

Douglas workers that jammed the shows at both cities saw their own handiwork in action—C-47s, the *Dauntlesses*, *Havocs*, Douglas-built *Liberator's* and *Flying Fortresses*.

Oklahoma City workers, right, inspect a "peep". Above, bazookas at Tulsa. Mrs. Bernice B. Birkel, Y505, whose son was killed on an Italy-bound transport spoke to the workers at Tulsa, and Mrs. Hattie Childers, of the C-47 fuselage assembly, mother of Sgt. Jack Childers, missing over Germany, spoke to the men and women of Oklahoma City. Both mothers led fellow workers in a pledge to "stay on the job and finish the job."

This is an excerpt about the *Tulsa Attacks!* performance from the August 1944 issue of the *Douglas Airview*. (Courtesy of Oklahoma City Air Logistics Center History Office.)

This is an aerial view of Skelly Stadium, where the *Tulsa Attacks!* show took place in June 1944. At upper right is the University of Tulsa campus, a barren-looking locale in comparison to its vast present-day spread. Originally known as Skelly Field, the stadium was built in 1930 with a 14,500-seat capacity. It was named for its primary benefactor, Tulsa oilman William Skelly. (Courtesy of the Beryl Ford Collection/Rotary Club of Tulsa, Tulsa City-County Library and Tulsa Historical Society.)

This beautiful image, taken from Lookout Mountain on Tulsa's West Side, was shot by noted local photographer Bob McCormack on the night of the *Tulsa Attacks!* show. McCormack took multiple shots and combined them in the darkroom to create this image. The spotlight illumination came from Skelly Stadium during the show. (Courtesy of the Bob McCormack photographic studio archive, Coll. No. 2008.049, Department of Special Collections and University Archives, McFarlin Library, University of Tulsa.)

Tulsa has had its share of exclusive country clubs over the years. Construction of the Oakhurst Club, now known as the Oaks Country Club, began in 1921, including an 18-hole golf course designed by landscape architect A.W. Tillinghast that catered to Tulsa's wealthy elite for decades. It is now the second-oldest golf course in Tulsa. (Courtesy of the Oklahoma Collection, Coll. No. 2006.012, Department of Special Collections and University Archives, McFarlin Library, University of Tulsa.)

The Philbrook Museum of Art at 2727 South Rockford Road was originally the home of oilman Waite Phillips, who donated it to the city in 1939. The grounds of the museum cover 23 acres, and the museum averages around 123,000 visitors per year. (Courtesy of the Oklahoma Collection, Coll. No. 2006.012, Department of Special Collections and University Archives, McFarlin Library, University of Tulsa.)

A remarkable aerial camera view of some of the forty-two million spending spectators, who annually visit our amusement zone.

The Exposition Center at Twenty-first Street and Yale Avenue, now known as the Tulsa Fairgrounds, held spectacular shows, even during wartime. The Royal American Show boasted the "World's Largest Midway" at this 1943 expo. (Courtesy of the Oklahoma Collection, Coll. No. 2006.012, Department of Special Collections and University Archives, McFarlin Library, University of Tulsa.)

This is a show program for the 1943 Tulsa State Fair. (Courtesy of the Oklahoma Collection, Coll. No. 2006.012, Department of Special Collections and University Archives, McFarlin Library, University of Tulsa.)

AMUSEMENT CORPORATION OF AMERICA

194_ PICTORIAL MAGAZINE

10¢

WORLD'S LARGEST MIDWAY

ROYAL AMERICAN

TULSA SHOWS 4 DAYS 4 ONLY

BARTON SHOW GROUNDS

STARTS MONDAY, SEPTEMBER 18

The wartime draft depleted the pool of professional sportsmen, leaving mostly second-stringers and, eventually, women's leagues to fill the void. The minor-league Tulsa Oilers mostly played at Oiler Park, which was located on Fifteenth Street and Sandusky Avenue. From 1933 to 1942, the Oilers played in the Texas League, but the league was shut down in 1943 because of the war and did not reopen again until 1946. The team moved to New Orleans in 1976. (Courtesy of the Oklahoma Collection, Coll. No. 2006.012, Department of Special Collections and University Archives, McFarlin Library, University of Tulsa.)

Oiler Park was always a popular spot for soldiers on leave. Here, two GIs enjoy a game with their dates. (Author's collection.)

Five

CIVIL DEFENSE AND COMMUNITY LIFE

America in the 1940s was all about organization. With the country's war-based economy, an emphasis on getting the job done was present at every school, business, and street corner. There were malingerers and war profiteers, and a black market did thrive despite wartime rationing, but these were generally the exceptions that proved the rule. Americans were expected to cut back on common staples like meat, sugar, and coffee. Gasoline was rationed, shifts in factories were long, and people, though frustrated, muddled through. President Roosevelt kept inflation from soaring through the Office of Price Administration, which set up a rationing system that regulated what was available to the public and when. It was not popular, and Roosevelt certainly took criticism for it, but it was a necessity, and the vast majority of the nation trusted him enough to elect him to unprecedented third and fourth terms in office. In an age filled with political polarization and rote adherence to party ideology, it is almost an alien concept to think that Americans were ever as united for common purpose as they were during World War II.

The organizations that helped foster this sense of organization and unity had offices across the nation, and some, like the Red Cross, were worldwide. Many were directly spawned by the war or immediately preceded it. But with the advent of war, the New Deal was partially phased out and replaced with organizations designed for wartime. Executives who understood industrial productivity and applied it to this new emphasis replaced the social reformists who once made up Roosevelt's cabinet.

The Office of Civilian Defense (OCD) was established in 1941 for the express purpose of coordinating with local and state governments to facilitate civilian participation and awareness of emergency and national defense programs. First Lady Eleanor Roosevelt wanted it to do even more, including expanded participatory roles for women and programs for public health and welfare. Interestingly, the OCD never had more than 75 salaried staff members but instead depended on a volunteer force of over 11 million Americans across 14,000 local defense councils and nine regional offices. Many have criticized the usefulness of such an organization, considering that many of the defensive plans drawn up were contingent upon the United States being directly attacked by Axis forces. Blackout drills, Civil Air Patrols (except for those in coastal areas), and emergency medical services for bombing victims all seemed frivolous and unnecessary once it became obvious that the war would not come to American shores. However, proponents argue that the OCD was useful for training communities to prepare and stockpile in the event of natural disasters, which was especially true for Tulsa. Tulsa's civil defense system proved its effectiveness when overseeing rescue operations during the flood of 1943, providing a wealth of relief and comfort to citizens left homeless and hungry after the rising waters breached the banks of the Arkansas River and flooded numerous residential neighborhoods.

The American Women's Voluntary Services (AWVS) began in 1940. The AWVS was a progressive front-runner in that it was open to all women, regardless of race and color, and was completely nonpartisan. Bundles for America was another nonprofit organization that served the needs of the military, sewing uniforms to fill government orders and providing clothing for families of servicemen. They also organized music rooms, libraries, and recreation centers on military bases.

The American Red Cross (ARC), which aided the Armed Forces extensively, was the best-known service organization. Among the numerous functions of the Red Cross, they prepared care packages for American troops in enemy POW camps and relieved burdens of understaffing by volunteering at hospitals. Those who went overseas provided support and morale by running mobile canteens and serving as "Donut Dollies," while others served aboard hospital ships, trains, and at mobile hospital camps.

Community activism often blossoms in institutions of education and spiritualism, and Tulsa's numerous schools, churches, civic organizations, and even scout troops contributed greatly to the war effort by volunteering and raising money for organizations like the Tulsa War and Community Chest.

This is Tulsa's oldest high school, Central High School, which originally opened in 1906 at Fourth Street and Boston Avenue and moved to a larger site (pictured) at Sixth Street and Cincinnati Avenue in 1917. The school closed in 1976, and this building now houses the offices of Public Service Company of Oklahoma. (Courtesy of the Oklahoma Collection, Coll. No. 2006.012, Department of Special Collections and University Archives, McFarlin Library, University of Tulsa.)

West Tulsa's Daniel Webster High School was a Depression-era WPA success. It was built in 1938 and remains in operation at 1919 West Fortieth Street. (Courtesy of the Oklahoma Collection, Coll. No. 2006.012, Department of Special Collections and University Archives, McFarlin Library, University of Tulsa.)

First Presbyterian Church
Tulsa, Oklahoma

MINISTERS
REV. EDMUND F. MILLER, D.D. · REV. ROY M. SMITH
REV. C. W. KERR, D.D., Pastor Emeritus.

The WPA also built Will Rogers High School at 3909 South Fifth Place in 1938. Many students in the school's inaugural graduating classes served in World War II. The school, with its distinct Art Deco design, was prominently featured in a 1942 issue of *LIFE* magazine and is listed on the National Register of Historic Places. (Courtesy of the Oklahoma Collection, Coll. No. 2006.012, Department of Special Collections and University Archives, McFarlin Library, University of Tulsa.)

Worship has always been a part of Tulsa's identity, and the First Presbyterian Church has been a community mainstay since its inception in the early 1880s. The church has been moved and rebuilt three times since it opened and is an example of Gothic architecture. During the 1921 race riot, First Presbyterian Reverend Charles William Kerr utilized the church's basement to house refugees from the destroyed Greenwood District. (Courtesy of the Oklahoma Collection, Coll. No. 2006.012, Department of Special Collections and University Archives, McFarlin Library, University of Tulsa.)

Christ the King Catholic Church, built in 1928 at 1520 South Rockford Avenue, has the unique claim of being the first church in the world to bear this name. It houses some of the best examples of stained glass in the United States. (Courtesy of the Oklahoma Collection, Coll. No. 2006.012, Department of Special Collections and University Archives, McFarlin Library, University of Tulsa.)

The largest Catholic church in Tulsa is Holy Family Cathedral at 122 West Eighth Street. Built in 1912, it was the highest structure in Tulsa until the construction of the Mayo Hotel in 1923. (Author's collection.)

FIFTIETH ANNIVERSARY
Boston Avenue Methodist Church
1893 - - - 1943

Boston Avenue United Methodist, which began in 1893, is one of Tulsa's oldest churches. The church's current building, a massive structure and a distinctive part of Tulsa's skyline, was designed in the 1920s and still stands at 1301 South Boston Avenue. This commemorative brochure is from the church's 50th anniversary celebration held in 1943. (Courtesy of the Oklahoma Collection, Coll. No. 2006.012, Department of Special Collections and University Archives, McFarlin Library, University of Tulsa.)

This is the former site of Temple Israel, reportedly the oldest synagogue in Oklahoma, at Fourteenth Street and Cheyenne Avenue. The building was abandoned and became derelict before the war and is now a burned-out shell. The synagogue's current location, at 2004 East Twenty-second Place, continues to serve Tulsans. (Courtesy of the Oklahoma Collection, Coll. No. 2006.012, Department of Special Collections and University Archives, McFarlin Library, University of Tulsa.)

One of the largest propositions on the minds of Tulsans in March 1942 was whether or not to accept the building of the Douglas bomber plant, as shown in this brochure. The construction of the plant proved to be of enormous economic importance to the city and the war effort. (Courtesy of the Oklahoma Collection, Coll. No. 2006.012, Department of Special Collections and University Archives, McFarlin Library, University of Tulsa.)

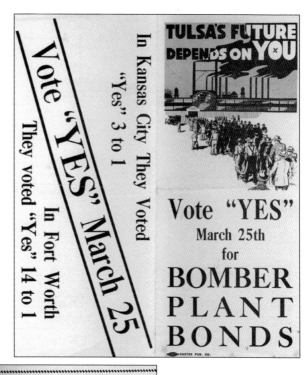

Vote "YES" March 25

In Kansas City They Voted "Yes" 3 to 1

In Fort Worth They voted "Yes" 14 to 1

TULSA'S FUTURE DEPENDS ON YOU

Vote "YES"
March 25th
for
BOMBER
PLANT
BONDS

PAYROLLS INSURE PROSPERITY

On Tuesday, March 25, the taxpayers of Tulsa will go to the polls to vote on the issuance of $750,000 in bonds, the proceeds of which will be used as follows:

1. For the acquisition of the necessary land for the giant $10,476,000 Airplane Bomber Assembly Plant to be built by the U. S. Government and operated by the Douglas Aircraft Co. Approximately .... $ 75,000.00
2. For the acquisition of the necessary land to expand Tulsa's Municipal Airport and create at least 7,000-foot runways in every direction. Approximately 175,000.00
3. For the extension of the municipally owned Spavinaw water system to the new plant and the area. Approximately 275,000.00
4. For the extension of sewers to the plant and area, and construction of a sewage disposal plant. Approximately 225,000.00

TOTAL $750,000.00

Mayor Veale's Pledge

"If there are any of the proceeds of the bond issue left after the requirements of the Government have been complied with, and after the airport has been expanded, that money remaining will be returned to the sinking fund to be used for the retirement of the bonds."

BOMBER PLANT FACTS

Contractors: Manhattan Construction Co., Muskogee, and Long Construction Co., Kansas City.
Price: $10,476,000.
Size: 4,000 by 320 feet for the main structure, plus additional footage for supplementary structures.
Plant area: 250-300 acres.
Total area: 1,000 acres.
Construction workers needed: Between 7,000 and 8,000.
Construction begins: This week.
Operation personnel expected: Between 15,000 and 17,000.
Estimated monthly operation pay roll: $1,450,000.

What This Bond Issue Will Cost You

This bond issue runs for only five years.
It will cost the taxpayer $1.74 on each $1,000 of his assessed property value for each year of the five.
For example, if you own a home valued at $4,000, your assessed valuation is approximately $2,000. Your homestead exemption is $1,000, leaving $1,000 on which you pay taxes. Thus, this new bond issue will cost you $1.74 per year. This small investment will make a large increase in your property value and create a better real estate market.

Why This Bond Issue Must Be Voted

Never before has Tulsa had opportunity knocking so loudly at her door—employment is now assured thousands of her citizens, both in building the new factory and in operating it, for 8,000 men will work on the construction and at least 10,000 in the operation of the plant.
The $17,400,000 annual payroll from the plant should result in a general overall increase of 15 per cent in Tulsa's business.
A 10 per cent increase in Tulsa's population is likely. This will fill Tulsa's vacant homes, make use of Tulsa's vacant store rooms and enable hundreds of Tulsa families to make some extra money by taking roomers.
"I am happy to advise and guarantee the taxpayer that the interest rate on the $750,000 Bond Issue will not exceed 1%. Due to the fact that we have paid off over $900,000 worth of City of Tulsa Bonds this fiscal year, I also guarantee the taxpayer that your tax rate will not be increased over 50c per thousand according to the assessed valuation of 1940."—MAYOR VEALE.

Anticipated Annual Payrolls of $17,400,000, and How the Money Probably Will Be Spent:

38% for Food	$6,612,000
19% for Shelter	3,306,000
13% for Clothing	2,262,000
6% for Utilities	1,044,000
24% for Miscl. Items	4,176,000

—From the New York Times.

THE BUYING POWER TURNOVER OF ANY DOLLAR IS FIVE TIMES, OR $87,000,000.

Oklahoma Has Been Lagging

Oklahoma lost population and business between 1930 and 1940, the business census showing it lost more business than any state in the Middle West, Southwest, or South. This plant will change that trend.
Tulsa has already lost thousands of workers to the defense industries in Corpus Christi, Wichita, Los Angeles, and North Texas. This plant will bring these men home, and thousands more with them.
Failure to vote the bond issue would be to lose the plant and then thousands more of Tulsa's workers would have to leave home to get jobs.
Joe Parkinson, County Treasurer, says: "No one will be hurt by this bond issue and every Tulsan will be benefited in some way by the location of the Bomber Assembly Plant here."
We are on the eve of an industrial advancement. If you are interested in your individual profit and if you are concerned in promoting the growth of our city, then the Bomber Assembly Plant for Tulsa should be your first objective. Smaller industries will follow in the wake of this great project.
Water, Sewers, and Land are all necessary to secure the Bomber Plant—Vote "YES" on all three items.

Tulsa Bombers For National Defense

This is the interior of the brochure calling for the construction of the Douglas bomber plant. Several defense workers had been lured away from Tulsa to pursue jobs in Texas, Los Angeles, and Kansas, and the construction of the plant brought most of them home. (Courtesy of the Oklahoma Collection, Coll. No. 2006.012, Department of Special Collections and University Archives, McFarlin Library, University of Tulsa.)

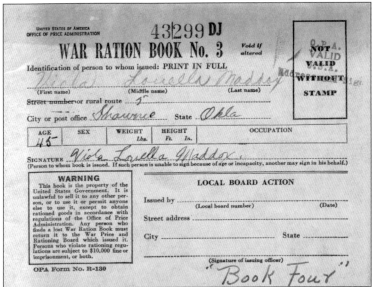

The Office of Price Administration oversaw the rationing of consumer goods to the public during World War II. Each family was allocated a certain number of ration books and stamps per month, depending on the size of the families. (Author's collection.)

Some people tried to buck the rationing system, as seen in this famous photograph of the arrest of Carol Ann Smith, of "Hex House" fame, in the summer of 1944. Smith told the ration board that she had eight people living in her house, including several children. When Tulsa police raided the house, they discovered that Smith was holding two women, Virginia Evans and Wiletta Horner, as virtual prisoners in her home. Circumstantial evidence linked Smith to at least three previous deaths, and the house became infamous for being cursed. The former site of the house, on Twenty-first Street across from Veterans Park, is now a favorite stop on local ghost tours. (Courtesy of *Tulsa World*.)

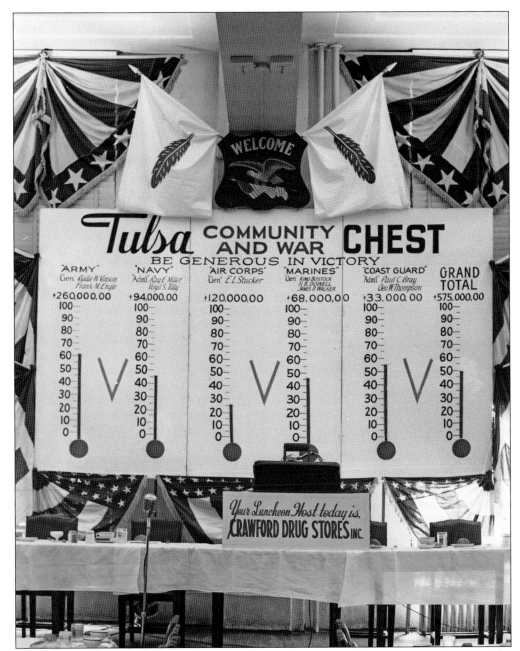

Conducting the business of war often required contributions and fundraising on the part of the community. This 1944 placard for the Tulsa Community and War Chest—sponsored by Crawford Drug, a chain that operated in Tulsa during the war—shows progress toward monetary goals. (Courtesy of the Beryl Ford Collection/Rotary Club of Tulsa, Tulsa City-County Library and Tulsa Historical Society.)

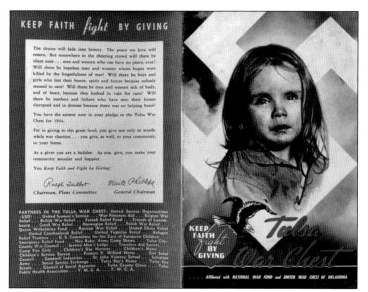

These are the front and back covers of the informational brochure produced to promote the Tulsa War Chest. Community organizations—including the USO, YMCA, and Goodwill Industries—united in the service of wartime fundraising. (Courtesy of the Oklahoma Collection, Coll. No. 2006.012, Department of Special Collections and University Archives, McFarlin Library, University of Tulsa.)

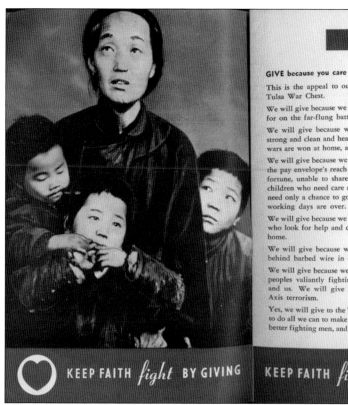

Part of the money raised through the Tulsa War Chest was allocated to China Relief. Atrocities committed by the Japanese appealed to American sympathies and were a big factor in the 1943 repeal of the Chinese Exclusion Act, which had barred Chinese immigration to the United States since the 1870s. (Courtesy of the Oklahoma Collection, Coll. No. 2006.012, Department of Special Collections and University Archives, McFarlin Library, University of Tulsa.)

Community groups like the YMCA and YWCA also benefited from the Tulsa War Chest, offering vocational training to young men and women. (Courtesy of the Oklahoma Collection, Coll. No. 2006.012, Department of Special Collections and University Archives, McFarlin Library, University of Tulsa.)

The Tulsa War Chest also raised money for public health organizations that filled the vacancies left by doctors and nurses serving overseas and funded groups that offered amenities and accommodations to soldiers in transit between postings. (Courtesy of the Oklahoma Collection, Coll. No. 2006.012, Department of Special Collections and University Archives, McFarlin Library, University of Tulsa.)

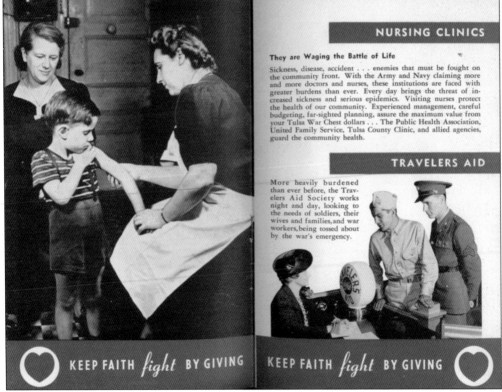

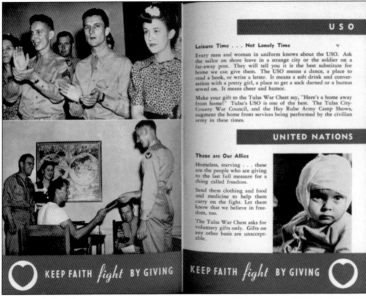

The war chest fundraising drives also helped fund the USO, offering troops on leave a place to unwind and socialize, and gave money to relief organizations like Bundles for America. (Courtesy of the Oklahoma Collection, Coll. No. 2006.012, Department of Special Collections and University Archives, McFarlin Library, University of Tulsa.)

One of the greatest contributions of the Tulsa War Chest was raising money for the relief of prisoners of war. While POWs in German camps received at least some of the amenities provided by such organizations, those captured by the Japanese seldom, if ever, did. Outrage at this fueled an intense hatred for Japan. (Courtesy of the Oklahoma Collection, Coll. No. 2006.012, Department of Special Collections and University Archives, McFarlin Library, University of Tulsa.)

The American Legion, a veterans' organization founded by returning World War I troops in 1919, has supported the military and veterans since its inception. This group poses atop a converted train car used by the French during World War I. The designation "40 hommes 8 chevaux" meant that the car could carry either 40 soldiers or eight horses. (Courtesy of the Beryl Ford Collection/Rotary Club of Tulsa, Tulsa City-County Library and Tulsa Historical Society.)

The American Women's Voluntary Services were more than just "jills of all trades." They worked with the Motor Transport Service, sold war bonds, organized scrap metal drives, harvested crops, and offered legal aid and emergency switchboard services anywhere they were needed. Tulsa's AWVS often coordinated with the Red Cross and OCD for fundraising events. (Courtesy of the Beryl Ford Collection/Rotary Club of Tulsa, Tulsa City-County Library and Tulsa Historical Society.)

Bigotry was a visible facet of American society in some corners during World War II. When the Tulsa Red Cross set up blood drives, posters like this reminded the public of the foolishness of such attitudes. (Courtesy of the Oklahoma Collection, Coll. No. 2006.012, Department of Special Collections and University Archives, McFarlin Library, University of Tulsa.)

Another example of community solidarity is demonstrated in this poster issued by the Institute for American Democracy, which decried bigotry in the workplace. The poster depicts workers in a steel foundry. (Courtesy of the Oklahoma Collection, Coll. No. 2006.012, Department of Special Collections and University Archives, McFarlin Library, University of Tulsa.)

Another community spirit poster addresses overt racism. This poster is unique and groundbreaking for the segregated 1940s, considering it actually depicts a black citizen among white ones. (Courtesy of the Oklahoma Collection, Coll. No. 2006.012, Department of Special Collections and University Archives, McFarlin Library, University of Tulsa.)

This poster issued by the Institute for American Democracy addressed children and racially charged questions. While these calls for social and racial tolerance were laudable, they arrived during a time when Japanese-Americans were interned in remote desert areas and Jim Crow segregation was an ironclad law in the South. It is also interesting to note that the posters circulated in Tulsa 20 years after the violent race riot of 1921. (Courtesy of the Oklahoma Collection, Coll. No. 2006.012, Department of Special Collections and University Archives, McFarlin Library, University of Tulsa.)

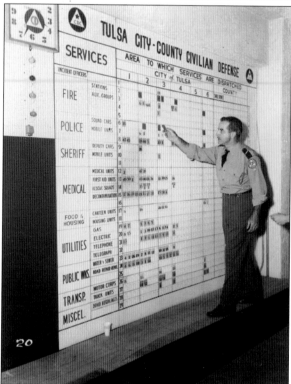

Civil defense meant intense community involvement. Civil defense volunteers served as aircraft spotters, auxiliary police, volunteer firefighters, rescue workers, medical personnel, and blackout wardens. (Courtesy of the Beryl Ford Collection/Rotary Club of Tulsa, Tulsa City-County Library and Tulsa Historical Society.)

Tulsa's Office of Civil Defense had a locally elected Defense Council overseeing operations. The OCD was temporarily deactivated in 1945 but revived during the Cold War. Though abolished in 1979, the primary functions of the OCD are now performed by the Federal Emergency Management Agency (FEMA). (Courtesy of the Beryl Ford Collection/Rotary Club of Tulsa, Tulsa City-County Library and Tulsa Historical Society.)

Tulsa's emergency organizations sprang into action when a massive flood in the summer of 1943 caused the Arkansas River to rise throughout vast areas of the city. (Courtesy of the Beryl Ford Collection/Rotary Club of Tulsa, Tulsa City-County Library and Tulsa Historical Society.)

Here, civil defense volunteers scramble to rescue those trapped by the 1943 flood along the Sand Springs line in Northwest Tulsa. (Courtesy of the Beryl Ford Collection/Rotary Club of Tulsa, Tulsa City-County Library and Tulsa Historical Society.)

This image may appear somewhat comical, however, the flood of 1943 was anything but. If not for swift action on the part of civil defense organizations, damage to the city could have been much worse. Here, civil defense leaders band together for community solidarity while standing in ankle-deep floodwaters. (Courtesy of the Beryl Ford Collection/Rotary Club of Tulsa, Tulsa City-County Library and Tulsa Historical Society.)

Six

THOSE WHO SERVED AND THEIR LEGACIES TODAY

Some people felt a calling to enter the service during World War II. For some, it was the desire to serve their country. For others, it was indignation at the Pearl Harbor attacks. Most old-timers, many of whom were not even 30 yet, had enlisted during the Depression to escape the hunger of those years. Some were in federalized National Guard units pressed into active service, while others waited for their draft numbers to come up. For others, it was "go into the Army or go to jail." Thousands of people from across the country came to Oklahoma to train at places like Camp Gruber, Fort Sill, Fort Reno, or the Navy WAVE facility in Stillwater.

Tulsa already had its military claim to fame. The gunboat USS *Tulsa*, launched in 1923, served in the South China Patrol and was among the last ships of the Asiatic fleet to escape the Japanese and find safety in Australia. More famous was the battleship USS *Oklahoma*, commissioned in 1916. The *Oklahoma* rescued refugees from the Spanish Civil War in 1936 but capsized during the Japanese attack at Pearl Harbor, taking 429 members of her crew with her as she rolled over. The *Oklahoma* never regained her initial glory. Her guns and superstructure were stripped for use on other ships, and her hull sank to the bottom of the Pacific while being towed back to the mainland for scrap in 1947.

Tulsans had a great deal of pride and worry for their sons, husbands, and boyfriends headed overseas. Many joined a National Guard unit, the 45th Infantry Division, made up of boys from New Mexico, Colorado, Arizona, and Oklahoma. This group of young men from the Sooner State were among the first Americans to witness the horrors of the Holocaust when the unit liberated Dachau concentration camp, discovering thousands of corpses.

It is a supreme irony that while Oklahoma boys were crushing the Third Reich, many Germans were enjoying the relative luxuries of POW camps across the state, most notably at Camp Gruber. Oklahoma always had a large German population, and captured *Wehrmacht* troops worked the area farms in the absence of sons in uniform.

An unlikely memorial to World War II stands outside Tulsa in the nearby community of Muskogee, where the USS *Batfish* (SS 310) submarine is on permanent display. After serving as a training vessel until the 1960s, she eventually made her way down the Arkansas River to her final berthing in May 1972. The *Batfish* has been there ever since and is one of the most accessible World War II monuments.

A number of Oklahomans who earned reputations had arguably closer ties to the state because they were Native Americans. Jake McNiece, of Indian descent, was a two-fisted, brawling paratrooper and pathfinder with the 506th Parachute Infantry Regiment, 101st Airborne. Charles Chibitty was a Comanche who served as a code talker in the 4th Infantry Division. Ernest Childers, born in the Tulsa suburb of Broken Arrow, was a Muscogee Creek and endured the hardships of Chilocco Indian School. As a lieutenant with the 45th Infantry Division, he single-handedly took out two German snipers, two machine-gun nests, and captured an artillery observer, winning the Congressional Medal of Honor.

The majority of Tulsans served in anonymity, did their duty, and waited, hoping they had the percentage points required for a quick discharge and return home. Many of them took advantage of the GI Bill, earning college degrees. They settled down, started families, and tried to live out the dream they fought so hard for.

In 2004, native Tulsan and World War II veteran Al Price helped establish the World War Two Veterans of Tulsa, a diverse group with veterans from every branch of service and theater of operations. The group gives presentations at local schools, often joining with historical reenactment groups. Sadly, meetings a mere six or seven years ago that had 45 people in attendance are dwindling. It is the same with the Last Man's Club, a Tulsa-based organization of Pearl Harbor survivors. When the last one is left alive, he'll pop the cork on a very expensive bottle they all pooled their money to buy and toast his absent friends.

Nearly 5,500 Oklahomans died during the war. This is a small percentage of the 500,000 Americans who gave their lives, and a miniscule percentage of the 52 million total deaths. The United States was fortunate in its distance and geography, as well as being the largest industrial nation in the world, with a population that the Axis powers could not hope to defeat in a sustained conflict.

Despite the advantages, America suffered. The resilience of the people of Tulsa and of every city is admirable beyond words. For good reason, they are called the "Greatest Generation."

Soldiers march into Manila, past the bodies of slain Japanese troops, during the campaign to take back the Philippines. Lifelong Tulsan and member of the "Last Man's Club" Leslie Crawley graduated from Central High School in 1936. He served with the 33rd Infantry Division and fought across New Guinea and the Philippines. Crawley entered Japan on September 20, 1945, becoming part of the Army of Occupation. (Courtesy of the Robert Pickering Photographs, Coll. No. 2010.100, Department of Special Collections and University Archives, McFarlin Library, University of Tulsa.)

The war in the Pacific theater took on a more brutal edge than in Europe, as Japanese troops seldom surrendered and often engaged in human-wave charges that, though startling to behold, often rendered a huge body count as they were cut down in droves by machine-gun fire. (Courtesy of the Robert Pickering Photographs, Coll. No. 2010.100, Department of Special Collections and University Archives, McFarlin Library, University of Tulsa.)

One of the US Army's chief artillery schools is at Fort Sill, Oklahoma. Many Tulsans who enlisted or drafted attended advanced training at Fort Sill. (Author's collection.)

This graduation photograph, taken just prior to America entering the war in 1941, shows Battery A, 27th Battalion, at Fort Sill—one of hundreds of such classes at this camp. (Author's collection.)

This is an aerial view from 1943 of the Camp Gruber cantonment outside Muskogee, Oklahoma. Constructed by Tulsa-based Manhattan Construction in 1942, the main post covered more than 260 acres and contained over 2,250 buildings. (Courtesy of Camp Gruber/National Archives.)

Camp Gruber, located southeast of Tulsa along Highway 165, is still active as a training camp for the National Guard. Here is one of the camp entrance signs, along with a lady who needs a ride. (Courtesy of Camp Gruber/National Archives.)

Female soldiers in the Women's Army Corps (WAC) line up for an official presidential visit to Camp Gruber on April 18, 1943. (Courtesy of Camp Gruber/National Archives.)

Troops assigned to armored units of the 88th Infantry Division await President Roosevelt's arrival. (Courtesy of Camp Gruber/National Archives.)

President Roosevelt is driven past troops lined up for review at Camp Gruber. (Courtesy of Camp Gruber/National Archives.)

The general public was largely unaware of President Roosevelt's crippling polio. When he visited Camp Gruber in 1943, accommodations were made so that the president could ride directly up to the podium via ramps on either end of the stage. (Courtesy of Camp Gruber/National Archives.)

Troops stationed at Camp Gruber could expect long, grueling endurance marches in the Oklahoma heat, as these troops from the 88th Division quickly learned. (Courtesy of Camp Gruber/National Archives.)

Troops from all over the country called Oklahoma home while training. An instructor from California teaches another from New York as he practices on the firing range with a .03 Springfield rifle. (Courtesy of Camp Gruber/National Archives.)

Advanced infantry training at Gruber tested a soldier's ability to withstand the stresses of combat. Here, a mortar squad encounters simulated artillery fire. (Courtesy of Camp Gruber/National Archives.)

Engineering battalions at Camp Gruber, like these from the 315th Engineering Company, learned to make pontoon bridges using wooden planks and rubber rafts. This exercise took place outside the camp, along Lake Greenleaf. (Courtesy of Camp Gruber/National Archives.)

No soldier left Camp Gruber without sufficient training in hand-to-hand combat, as demonstrated by two sergeants from the 807th Tank Destroyer Battalion. (Courtesy of Camp Gruber/National Archives.)

In this 1943 image, members of the 88th Signal Company's Radio Squad work in the field during training at Camp Gruber. (Courtesy of Camp Gruber/National Archives.)

Chemical warfare training was necessary, considering it was unknown whether or not the Germans would use poison gas against Allied troops, as they had during World War I. Thankfully, these chemical covers were never used in combat. (Courtesy of Camp Gruber/National Archives.)

Camp Gruber also had facilities for training K9 units, which were used by military police to guard high-security areas and prisoner enclosures. Here, Pfc. Ray Johns of Dallas, Texas, agitates a guard dog in training. (Courtesy of Camp Gruber/National Archives.)

One thing every soldier in every camp across the country learned was the importance of keeping equipment clean and in good working order. (Courtesy of Camp Gruber/National Archives.)

These 88th Division "Blue Devils" demonstrate the ambiguities of Army food and field kitchens. (Courtesy of Camp Gruber/National Archives.)

Inevitably, training came to an end, and farewells ensued as troops left Oklahoma to head overseas. This troop train carried soldiers to a point of embarkation on the way to the Pacific. (Courtesy of Camp Gruber/National Archives.)

After seeing combat in Europe, troops from the 86th "Blackhawk" Division came to Camp Gruber, only to leave Oklahoma shortly thereafter when they were redeployed to the Pacific in August 1945. Fortunately, the Japanese surrendered before they arrived. (Courtesy of Camp Gruber/National Archives.)

Many Tulsa women who gravitated toward the military during World War II found themselves working jobs they would never have envisioned as civilians. In this image, mechanic Ethel Woodward services a carburetor at Camp Gruber. (Courtesy of Camp Gruber/National Archives.)

Other women, such as these telephone operators, worked traditional clerical and office jobs at Camp Gruber. (Courtesy Camp Gruber/Pauline Moore Shriver collection.)

The 42nd "Rainbow" Division was deactivated at the conclusion of World War I. In this photograph, a "Great War" veteran ceremoniously acts as a witness to the division's reactivation at Camp Gruber in July 1943. (Courtesy of Camp Gruber/National Archives.)

Not all troops who trained in Oklahoma survived to tell the tale. Here are members of the 969th Battalion of the 333rd Artillery Regiment, a segregated Negro unit that trained at Camp Gruber. (Courtesy of Camp Gruber/National Archives.)

Members of a battery from the 333rd, known as the "Wereth 11," were executed by SS troops outside of Wereth, Belgium, on December 17, 1944, during the Battle of the Bulge. Their deaths coincided with the larger Malmedy Massacre that took place at the same time. (Courtesy of Camp Gruber/National Archives.)

This is a guard tower overlooking the German POW compound at Camp Gruber. The camp operated from 1943 to 1946 and was designed to hold more than 5,750 prisoners. (Courtesy of Camp Gruber/Pauline Moore Shivers collection.)

German POWs at Gruber built their own entertainment pavilion. In this c. 1944 photograph, they are staging a comedy/variety show. (Courtesy of Camp Gruber/National Archives.)

German POWs received excellent treatment and were encouraged to be productive—they undertook many monuments and beautification projects. Out of necessity, some POWs were kept segregated from others. This monument, which translates to "My Honor is Loyalty," was built by SS prisoners. These men were heavily indoctrinated in National Socialist ideology, and their fanaticism often continued after capture. Reprisals against prisoners thought to be traitorous—such as the murder of Johannes Kunz at the POW camp in Tonkawa, Oklahoma—often required keeping them in a separate enclosure. (Courtesy of Camp Gruber/National Archives.)

One of the POW work projects was this massive drainage culvert, which is still in existence at Camp Gruber to this day and is visible near the camp's main gates. (Courtesy of Camp Gruber/National Archives.)

Virginia Rado Curnutt (foreground, left), a longtime Tulsa resident, served overseas with the American Red Cross as a "Donut Dolly" with the USAAF 8th Air Force, 56th, and 257th Fighter Groups. (Courtesy of the Keith Myers collection.)

GIs with the 802nd Tank Destroyer Battalion in Europe enjoy doughnuts and coffee delivered by Virginia Rado Curnutt and the Red Cross in one of their iconic donut carts. (Courtesy of the Keith Myers collection.)

Ray Amstutz served as a T-4 sergeant and engineer with the 6th Army in the Philippines, New Guinea, and Occupied Japan. A lifelong Tulsan, Amstutz graduated from Will Rogers High School in 1941. He poses beneath Gen. Douglas MacArthur's personal B-17 transport, the *Bataan*. (Courtesy of Ray Amstutz.)

The author (left) is pictured here with Ray Amstutz (center) and Kevin O'Keefe at the 2010 Veterans Day Parade in Tulsa. Amstutz marches in the parade every year in the same uniform and boots he came home in after being discharged in 1945. (Author's collection.)

Just after the surrender of Japan, American engineers in Tokyo erect 10,000-pound oil storage tanks manufactured by Tulsa business National Tank Company. (Courtesy of Ray Amstutz.)

Sitting atop the oil storage tank pictured above, Ray Amstutz (squatting, left) and two other GIs relax and supervise as newly surrendered Japanese soldiers use wrenches to finish constructing the top deck. (Courtesy of Ray Amstutz.)

Here, Ray Amstutz (left) and fellow Will Rogers High School graduate Bill Turner pose in front of Emperor Hirohito's palace in Tokyo in 1945. (Courtesy of Ray Amstutz.)

Just prior to the invasion of Leyte, Pvt. Bob Brown repairs a pump manufactured in Tulsa. This device was designed to pump 100-octane fuel to ships waiting offshore at the invasion's embarkation point. Because of Private Brown's quick thinking and diligence, the invasion schedule was kept, and he went from private to sergeant overnight. (Courtesy of Ray Amstutz.)

Dewey F. and Marge Wilson lived at 806 South Indianapolis Avenue in Tulsa when Dewey was drafted in 1942. While Dewey went to signal corps training at Camp Crowder in Neosho, Missouri, and later served in the North African and Italian campaigns, Marge worked as a nurse at Morningside Hospital (later Hillcrest Hospital). (Courtesy of Dewey Wilson Jr.)

The "Thunderbirds" of the 45th Infantry first saw action in Sicily in 1943. They gained fame as the "Rock of Anzio" for their defiance in the face of relentless German attacks. In April 1945, they liberated the Nazi concentration camp at Dachau, with help from a contingent of the 42nd, another division that trained in Oklahoma. Their exploits are enshrined at the 45th Infantry Division Museum in Oklahoma City. (Courtesy of Kevin O'Keefe.)

Kay McCurdy, another longtime Tulsa resident, served in the US Army Nurse Corps. In this photograph from Fort Sill, McCurdy is at right; the other two nurses are unidentified. (Courtesy of Keith Myers collection.)

Ironically, war has often spurred blossoming romances. Kay McCurdy is pictured here at Fort Sill with her husband, Capt. Fred McCurdy. The couple lived in Tulsa the rest of their lives. Fred died in 1992 and Kay in 2007. (Courtesy of Keith Myers collection.)

Identical twins Clyde and Donald MacMasters hailed from the Tulsa suburb of Sapulpa. Both joined the Navy and served as naval aviators. (Courtesy of Keith Myers.)

While both MacMasters served as Navy pilots, it is doubtful they served together. Following the tragedy of the five Sullivan brothers dying together aboard the USS *Juneau* in November 1942, the "No Sibling" rule, officially known as the Sole Survivor Policy, enacted in 1948 does not allowed siblings to serve in the same units together. The directive also precludes those who have already lost family members to combat from being enlisted. (Courtesy of Keith Myers collection.)

Identical Twins Take Air Training Together

—Official U. S. Navy Phot

This is not done with mirrors. What looks like a mirror this picture is simply a pane of glass separating identical twin Ensigns Clyde V. and Donald H. MacMasters.

Another World War II attraction is the USS *Batfish*, shown here in its permanent dry-dock berthing in Muskogee, Oklahoma. (Courtesy of Kevin O'Keefe.)

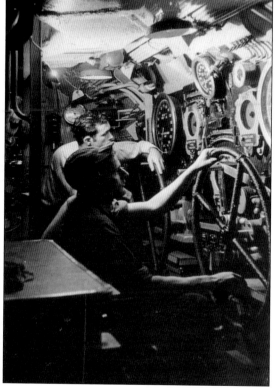

In this 1944 image, sailors on combat patrol work in the control room aboard the USS *Batfish* somewhere in the Pacific Ocean. (Courtesy of the USS *Batfish* War Memorial and Museum.)

Here, a torpedo is lowered into the forward torpedo room of the *Batfish* sometime in 1943 or 1944. Torpedoes were slid down tubes and then rolled into container racks, where they were secured until use. Sailors at this duty station slept directly over the explosives. (Courtesy of the USS *Batfish* War Memorial and Museum.)

This is the crew of the USS *Batfish* in 1944. The *Batfish* sank nine Japanese vessels and earned a Presidential Unit Citation and six Battle Stars for her service. (Courtesy of the USS *Batfish* War Memorial and Museum.)

Today, the USS *Batfish* is partially maintained by a group of living history reenactors (seen here) who preserve the memory of its wartime crew. They are assigned duty stations and give guided tours of the boat two to three times per year. In July 2010, the long-lost mast of the battleship USS *Oklahoma* was donated to the USS *Batfish* War Memorial and Museum after being discovered in Pearl Harbor. (Author's collection.)

In this 2008 photograph, historical reenactor Bob Hartung (left) poses with veteran paratrooper Jake McNiece. McNiece had four combat jumps during the war, including at Normandy and Holland. He led pathfinders into Bastogne during the Battle of the Bulge in December 1944, leading C-47 transports that dropped supplies to the surrounded 101st Airborne Division. He jumped again in March 1945 during Operation Varsity in Germany. After the war, McNiece returned to Oklahoma and served as a postman until his retirement. He has written a memoir of his wartime exploits called *The Filthy Thirteen*. (Author's collection.)

Al Price (left), one of the founders of the World War II Veterans of Tulsa, stands with Charles Chibitty, a Comanche and native Oklahoman who served as a code talker in the European theater. The Comanche language had never been written down and, thus, confounded German forces eavesdropping on American radio frequencies. Chibitty served with the 6th Army Signal Company of the 4th Infantry Division. Chibitty was the last surviving Comanche code talker until his death in 2005. He is buried at Floral Haven Memorial Gardens in east Tulsa. Price was born in Tulsa and drafted in 1942. He trained at Fort Sill and served with the 2nd Infantry Division, fighting through Normandy, France, Belgium, and Germany. (Courtesy of Kevin O'Keefe.)

First, second, and third from left are Al Price, Kevin O'Keefe, and Paul Andert with other, unidentified members of World War II Veterans of Tulsa and the author (second from right) in the fall of 2008 to open an exhibit of World War II militaria at the Sand Springs Cultural and Historical Museum. Sgt. Paul Andert, formerly of the 41st Armored Infantry, wrote a memoir of his wartime experiences entitled *Unless You Have Been There*. (Author's collection.)

Cpl. Bill Arter, famous as the "Boogie Woogie Bugle Boy" from the Andrews Sisters' song, is pictured here (center) in 2008 with the author (left) and his son, Nathan, at the annual Marine Corps League's Medal of Honor Recipients event at Tulsa's Veterans Park at Twenty-first Street and Boulder Park Drive. Corporal Arter earned a spot with the St. Louis Cardinals but was drafted before he could report for spring training. His proficiency as a musician came to the Andrews Sisters' attention, but Arter's true fame came when he won five Bronze Stars as an Army medic and celebrated his 21st birthday by storming the beaches at Normandy on D-Day. He moved to Tulsa after the war and lived there for 52 years. Arter died in 2009. (Author's collection.)

BIBLIOGRAPHY

Butler, William J. *Tulsa 75, A History of Tulsa, Oklahoma*. Tulsa, OK: Metropolitan Tulsa Chamber of Commerce, 1974.

Collias, Joe G. *Frisco Power: Locomotives and Trains of the St. Louis–San Francisco Railway, 1903–1953*. Springfield, MO: The Frisco Railroad Museum, 1997.

Colman, Penny. *Rosie The Riveter: Women Working on the Home Front in World War II*. New York: Crown Publishing, 1995.

Cornelius, Jerry L. *Historic Photos of Tulsa*. New York: Turner Publishing Co., 2007.

de Quesada, Alejandro. *The US Home Front 1941–45*. Oxford, UK: Osprey Publishing, 2008.

Everly-Douze, Susan, and Terrell Lester. *Tulsa Times, A Pictorial History: Coming of Age*. Wenatchee, WA: World Publishing Co., 1988.

Serling, Robert J. *When the Airlines Went to War*. New York: Kensington Books, 1997.

Discover Thousands of Local History Books
Featuring Millions of Vintage Images

Arcadia Publishing, the leading local history publisher in the United States, is committed to making history accessible and meaningful through publishing books that celebrate and preserve the heritage of America's people and places.

Find more books like this at
www.arcadiapublishing.com

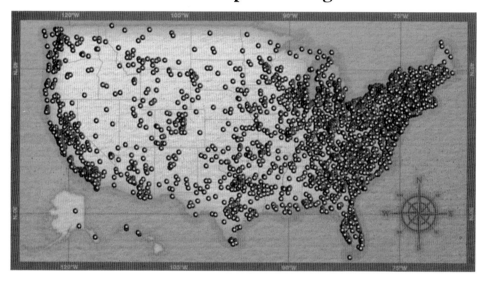

Search for your hometown history, your old stomping grounds, and even your favorite sports team.

Consistent with our mission to preserve history on a local level, this book was printed in South Carolina on American-made paper and manufactured entirely in the United States. Products carrying the accredited Forest Stewardship Council (FSC) label are printed on 100 percent FSC-certified paper.

MADE IN THE